KÖNIGS ERLÄUTERUNGEN SPEZIAL

Textanalyse und Interpretation zu

Tom Franklin

CROOKED LETTER, CROOKED LETTER

Patrick Charles

Analyse | Interpretation in englischer Sprache

Zitierte Ausgabe:

Franklin, Tom: *Crooked Letter, Crooked Letter*. Stuttgart: Ernst Klett Sprachen, 2017.

Note: All page references are to the Klett English Edition of the novel (ISBN 978-3-12-579900-4) and refer to the page and line numbers: for example, 191.25 is line 25 on page 191.

Über den Autor dieser Erläuterung:

Patrick Charles wurde 1973 in Bournemouth, Südengland, geboren und studierte englische Literatur an der Universität von Newcastle. 1993 zog er nach Berlin, wo er eine Ausbildung zum Buchhändler machte und zehn Jahre lang als Buchhändler arbeitete. Seit 2004 ist er als freiberuflicher Autor von Schulbüchern und Lernhilfen und als Übersetzer im Kulturbereich tätig. Er lebt mit seiner Familie in Berlin.

1. Auflage 2018

ISBN: 978-3-8044-3128-0

PDF: 978-3-8044-5128-5, EPUB: 978-3-8044-4128-6

© 2018 by Bange Verlag GmbH, 96142 Hollfeld

Alle Rechte vorbehalten!

Titelabbildung: Old pump station on Route 66 © forcdan/fotolia.com

Druck und Weiterverarbeitung: Tiskárna Akcent, Vimperk

1. FOREWORD – AT A GLANCE

This study guide to Tom Franklin's *Crooked Letter, Crooked Letter* is designed to provide an easy-to-use overview of the structure, context, themes and characters of the novel. Here is a quick rundown of the most important points.

Part 2 takes a brief look at Tom Franklin and his career.

⇨ S. 9
→ Franklin was born in Alabama in 1963. His career as a writer has been defined by the region of the country in which he was born and has always lived.

⇨ S. 10
→ *Crooked Letter* is a crime thriller about two boyhood friends who are in fact half-brothers. Franklin ist closely associated with the American South.

Part 3 offers analyses and interpretations of the novel.

Crooked Letter – Origins and sources

⇨ S. 16
Franklin is a Southern writer: all his published works have been concerned with the history and culture of the American South. *Crooked Letter* was published in 2010 and was his third and to date most successful novel.

Summaries

⇨ S. 18
Two young boys, Larry and Silas, become friends despite social and family pressure (Larry is white, Silas black) in rural Mississippi in the late 1970s. A girl they are both connected to, Cindy Walker, disappears, feared dead, and suspicion falls on Larry.
Twenty-five years later, Larry is an outcast in the area, and Silas is now a police officer, investigating the disappearance of a lo-

cal girl, Tina Rutherford. Larry is again a suspect, even after he is found shot and badly wounded in his own home. Silas investigates the crime and is forced to re-examine his own history, and to acknowledge the secrets he has been keeping about Cindy. He had been with her on the night she disappeared and he could have saved Larry from the suspicion which destroyed his family and his life. While investigating the past, Silas also discovers that he and Larry are half-brothers. Silas is badly injured in a showdown with the man who shot Larry and killed Tina. After Silas has confessed about the events of 1982, he and Larry can begin to mend their friendship.

Structure

The novel is concerned with events from the past and their effect on, and reflection in, events occurring in the present day. The narrative takes place in the two time periods, with some chapters taking place entirely in the past, and characters often slipping into long memories which reveal the secrets and events of 25 years ago.

⇨ S. 31

Characters

The arrangement of the characters in *Crooked Letter* is a little more complex than in a less chronologically complex novel.

⇨ S. 52

Larry Ott

⇨ S. 52

→ Larry is an outcast and a loner who comes from a local family.

Silas Jones

⇨ S. 55

→ Silas investigates the crimes in the novel and has to acknowledge his guilt for having ruined Larry's life.

2.1 Biography

2. TOM FRANKLIN: LIFE & WORKS

2.1 Biography

YEAR	PLACE	EVENT	AGE
1963	Dickinson, Alabama	Born on 7th of July in the tiny community (400–500 citizens), Franklin grew up as a huge fan of comic books and pulp fiction (science fiction, horror, fantasy, Tarzan stories, etc.) and was not a good student at school.	Up to age 18
1981	Mobile, Alabama	The family moved, and Franklin attended the University of South Alabama, where he worked many menial jobs and took nine years to graduate.	18
1994	Selma, Alabama	Taught for a year at the famous all-black Selma University.	31
1998	Fayetteville, Arkansas	He graduated from the University of Arkansas with an M.F.A. after four years which he really enjoyed, during which he also met his future wife Beth Ann.	35
1999		First work published, the story collection *Poachers*	36
2003		First novel published, *Hell at the Breech*	40
2006		*Smonk* is published, cementing his reputation as a regional writer	43
2010		*Crooked Letter, Crooked Letter* is published to widespread acclaim and great commercial success	47
2013		*The Titled World* is published, a novel Franklin co-wrote with his wife	50
2017		Tom Franklin is currently an associate professor at the University of Mississippi.	54

Thomas Gerald Franklin (* 1963) © Ulf ANDERSEN/ GAMMA-RAPHO/ laif

2.2 Contemporary Background

SUMMARY

Whether he is writing crime fiction or historical novels, Tom Franklin is a regional writer who is closely associated with the American South, specifically the states Alabama and Mississippi. The traditions, lifestyles and landscapes of the South feature prominently in his writing.

The South

The southern states of the USA are very different from the North. Traditional ways of life which were associated for generations with natural factors like different kind of agriculture (the plantations, for example) and the very different climate are combined with historical, political and social factors including slavery, segregation, the American Civil War, widespread religious intensity and a lot of rural poverty. Industrialisation and urbanisation had been northern phenomena long before they began affecting the South.

Southern identity

Franklin addresses many issues of Southern identity and life in *Crooked Letter*, including **racial dynamics**, the coherence and claustrophobia of small rural communities, and **social problems** like drugs, alcoholism and poverty. He also makes efforts to **portray the languid atmosphere** of the hot and humid climate, and there is a strong awareness of beauty in his descriptions of the landscapes of the South.

Chicago

North America, Illinois

Chicago has many nicknames, including the "Windy City" – referring to its chilly and raw climate – and the "City of the Big Shoulders", which is a line taken from Carl Sandburg's poem *Chicago* (1916)

2.2 Contemporary Background

and reflects the city's strong working-class and industrial identity. In *Crooked Letter*, Alice and Silas move from Chicago to Mississippi, which is for Silas like a **different world**. When Silas talks to Cindy about Chicago he describes an exciting place with raw weather, access to the highest level of national sports, great pizza and much more – a lively, stimulating environment, full of noise and pressure, very different from the slow and quiet rural world of Chabot and Fulsom (p. 243).

Race

Race is a huge issue in American history and culture, and while it is a factor throughout the entire country and throughout all social strata and demographics, it is historically particularly relevant to the Southern states, including Mississippi, where the novel is set.

Slavery and institutionalised **white supremacy** (the conviction that white people are fundamentally better than dark-skinned people) were defining features of Southern society for many years. The American Civil War has complex origins, but one of the major factors was the push to abolish slavery.

Racial segregation

The Civil Rights Movement of the 1960s had many of its defining moments occur in the South, where racial segregation was widespread and efforts to maintain the white supremacist status quo were fiercer and more oppressive than in the North. In a secretive shadowy world, **the institutional racism** which enforced segregated schools, bathrooms, buses and drinking fountains was accompanied by mob violence and the secret society **Ku Klux Klan**. The KKK was first formed in the 1860s to overthrow the Republic following the Civil War. The white supremacist identity of the Klan has remained its defining feature throughout the years. The KKK is a secret society, but members are famous for their distinctive uniform of white robes with pointed white hoods. The Klan has

2.2   Contemporary Background

Grave of 14-year-old Emmett Till, lynched by a white man.
© picture alliance/ AP Photo

been responsible for countless murders, lynchings and assaults on African-Americans and civil rights activists.

Silas had virtually no contact with white people when he was growing up in a peaceful all-black neighbourhood in Chicago (131.8–21). It was only when he came to Mississippi that he encountered white people who would openly call blacks the N-word. As an adult, Silas sees the effects of structural racism, for example when he looks at the courthouse and sees exclusively white lawyers and exclusively black defendants (174.4–6).

Class and social status

"White trash"

The South maintained an almost feudal social system far into the modern era, with powerful, dynastic landowners who ran their vast estates like medieval aristocratic properties, complete with succes-

2.2 Contemporary Background

sive generations of servants and, for a long period, slave labour. In *Crooked Letter*, the clearest example of class and social tensions is combined with racial issues in the idea of "white trash", specifically **Wallace Stringfellow and the Walker family**. These are white people who are at the very bottom of the social hierarchy, poor, uneducated, unskilled, unemployed, and often associated with drug addiction, alcoholism and domestic abuse. We can see in the character of Wallace how a lifetime of being treated like dirt can make you believe it at some point ("I ain't worth a shit", 283.10), but the combination of this sense of worthlessness with Wallace's emotional and psychological problems makes him a dangerous character. Cindy Walker on the other hand has also been subject to contempt and abuse throughout her young life, but she wants to escape and find a better life.

Religion

Religion in the Deep South has an interesting and diverse history. There is a long tradition of Protestantism, but the predominant denomination is the Southern Baptist Convention. There are also many Methodists.

Larry and Ina: Hunger for religion

Religion plays a minor role in *Crooked Letter*. Larry is a believer, and Wallace's first memories of Larry are of him in a church. Larry and his mother feel a genuine hunger for religion and must search for congregations which will accept them after Larry becomes the main suspect in the disappearance of Cindy Walker. They are Baptists.

2.3 Notes on other works

SUMMARY

Crooked Letter, Crooked Letter was Franklin's third novel, and is his most successful and famous work.

Works	Publication year
Poachers (short story collection)	1999
Hell at the Breech	2003
Smonk	2006
Crooked Letter, Crooked Letter	2010
The Tilted World	2013

Poachers

His first published work, this collection of short stories won a major prize in the field of crime fiction (the Edgar Award for Best Mystery Short Story).

Hell at the Breech and *Smonk*

His first two novels are historical novels, both examples of regional fiction, as they are set in Alabama. *Hell at the Breech*[1], his debut, was based on actual historical events. *Smonk* is a wildly over-the-top novel about a brutal rapist and his path of destruction, intended in part as a reaction against or parody of the excessively masculine Southern fiction of established writers like Cormac McCarthy (famous for novels like *Blood Meridian* – published 1985).

---

[1] German Translation: *Die Gefürchteten*. Heyne Verlag, 2005. Translated by Wolfgang Müller.

2.3 Notes on other works

Smonk

has recently been translated into German for the first time and has been receiving a lot of attention for its grotesque, energetic humour and brutality[2].

The Tilted World

Co-written with his wife, this is another historical, regional novel, set in Mississippi in 1927.

---

2 German Translation: *Smonk: Die Stadt der Witwen*. Verlag PULP MASTER, 2017. Translated by Nikolaus Stingl.

1 FORWORD –
   AT A GLANCE

2 TOM FRANKLIN:
   LIFE & WORK

3 ANALYSES AND
   INTERPRETATIONS

3.   ANALYSES AND INTERPRETATIONS

3.1 Origins and sources

SUMMARY

Tom Franklin is widely considered to be a regional, and specifically Southern writer. All of his published work has been set
in Mississippi or Alabama, and the region and his experiences
there have shaped his work as a writer.

"To write a story, you have to get the details right. You have to
convince a reader you know what you're talking about."[3]

(Tom Franklin)

Biographical
traces

Franklin's personal background in the region and his familiarity with
the life, landscape, history, people and feel of the South means that
there are **traces of his life and experience in his work**. This is also
true of *Crooked Letter*: for example, like Larry, he grew up with a
father who ran a car repair workshop in a tiny rural community.

He mentions in interviews how much autobiographical detail has
slipped into *Crooked Letter*: "the character of Silas "32" Jones is very
loosely based on the sole police officer of the hamlet of Dickinson,
Alabama, where I grew up"[4] and "I used a lot of autobiographical
stuff for Larry, the mechanic"[5]. These **autobiographical details** include Larry's reading habits – when asked in an interview who his

---

3   https://www.mswritersandmusicians.com/mississippi-writers/tom-franklin
4   https://www.amazon.com/Crooked-Letter-Novel/dp/0060594667/ref=ntt_at_ep_dpi_1
5   Ibid.

3.1 Origins and sources

favourite writers were and are, Franklin says, "I loved Stephen King and Edgar Rice Burroughs as a kid"[6].

His **roots in the South** have shaped him as a writer:

"So, yes, the south's made me the writer I am. It taught me to listen to the cadences and rhythms of speech, and to notice the landscape. It also has this defeated feel, a lingering of old sin, that makes it sweet in a rotting kind of way. Much of it is poor, much is rural, and that's an interesting combination, a deep well for stories."[7]

In the same interview, Franklin talks briefly about the origins of the novel: "I'd been wanting to write about a small town police officer, and I'd long had the image of a loner mechanic in my mind. When I put the two together, the story began to form."

This comment reinforces the impression many readers of *Crooked Letter* have that this is primarily a character-driven novel, and, despite the plot, only **secondarily a crime thriller**.

Character-driven novel

---

6   https://www.mswritersandmusicians.com/mississippi-writers/tom-franklin
7   https://www.amazon.com/Crooked-Letter-Novel/dp/0060594667/ref=ntt_at_ep_dpi_1

3.2 Summaries

SUMMARY

Two young boys, Larry and Silas, become friends in rural Mississippi in the late 1970s. A girl, Cindy Walker, disappears, feared dead, and suspicion falls on Larry.

Twenty-five years later, Larry is an outcast in the area, and Silas is now a police officer, investigating the disappearance of a local girl, Tina Rutherford. Larry is again a suspect, even after he is found shot and badly wounded in his own home. Silas investigates the crime and is forced to re-examine his own history. After Silas has confessed about the events of 1982, he and Larry can begin to mend their friendship.

What follows in this section is a brief chapter-by-chapter summary of the novel. Some of the chapters are based entirely or largely in the past, as the novel covers two different periods (1979–1982 and two weeks in 2007), and these flashbacks are indicated in the summaries.

one

Intruder shoots
Larry Ott

The novel starts with Larry Ott, a 41-year old man who lives alone in his parents' house. He wakes up and goes about his morning routine, looking after his chickens, and heads off to work in his father's car repair workshop, Ottomotive. On the way he gets a call from his mother, who is in a nursing home, saying that she would like to see him. He heads back home. When he walks into his house he is ambushed by an intruder wearing an old zombie mask which Larry has had since he was a boy. The intruder shoots him and then watches him bleeding out on the kitchen floor.

3.2 Summaries

two

Police Constable Silas "32" Jones is patrolling when he sees an unusually large number of buzzards – carrion eater birds – hovering over an area of woodland. He investigates, hoping/fearing that he will find the corpse of a missing girl, Tina Rutherford. Instead he finds the body of Morton "M&M" Morrisette in a swamp. M&M was a local marijuana dealer with whom Silas had played baseball and been good friends in high school.

Local detective and investigator Roy French arrives, followed by other officials, including Silas' girlfriend Angie, an EMT (emergency medical technician).

M&M was murdered

Later, back in the office he shares with Miss Voncille, the city clerk, Silas is visited by French, who says that he had visited Larry Ott regarding the missing Rutherford girl. Silas follows up on a report that a rattlesnake has been found in someone's mailbox. The mailbox belongs to a woman named Irina who shares a house with two other divorcees in a run-down area populated by poor whites.

Silas is doing his shift directing traffic later that day when he receives an ominous phone call from Angie, who is now at Ott's house.

three

This chapter is a flashback, beginning in March 1979. Larry recalls his father driving him to school one freezing cold morning. They see Silas and his mother, Alice, waiting by the road and pick them up. Familiarity between Larry's father and Alice Jones is implied. Larry's mother seems surprised and a little suspicious when he tells her about it later when she picks him up from school. This is repeated for days. Larry's mother quizzes him about the woman and how his father behaves with her. She drives Larry to school one day and it is obvious she and Alice know each other: She gives the

Jones' two second hand winter coats and makes a bitter comment before driving off and leaving them standing in the freezing cold.

Larry goes to find Silas in the woods, where the Jones family lives in a cabin. He seems to want to be friends with the other boy. He finds Silas, teaches him how to shoot, lends him a rifle and then leaves his gloves for the boy as well.

four

Larry tried to call Silas on the phone

Back to the present: On the phone to Silas, Angie describes briefly what she has found at Larry's place. Silas goes to investigate and is reminded of having been there once before when he and Larry were friends. French arrives and they examine the crime scene together (Larry is in hospital, badly wounded but not dead). After examining Ott's house, Silas returns home to find that Larry had tried to call him earlier that day, leaving a message on his answer machine.

five

> This very significant chapter shows how important Silas was for Larry, how lonely and withdrawn Larry is, and how un-pleasant and dangerous both Carl Ott and his friend and neigh-bour Cecil Walker are. It also shows the reader one of the two events (the fight – the other being the disappearance of Cindy Walker) which permanently changed the course of Larry's life.

Another chapter set in the past, this one describes events later in the year Silas and Larry first met, 1979, leading up to Carl forcing them to fight over the borrowed rifle. Silas beats Larry, who then calls him "n****r", changing their relationship for ever.

3.2 Summaries

six

> This chapter is divided between the present day and a substantial section containing Silas' recollections of his childhood and his journey with his mother from Chicago to Chabot.

Silas investigates further in Larry Ott's life. He goes to Ott's garage and then back to his house to look for further clues as to what has happened. He finds small pieces of glass and the butt of a joint. Being in Ott's house triggers memories of his childhood.

Silas remembers his early life in Chicago, and how, after his mother's boyfriend had been arrested and then gone on the run, he and his mother had left Chicago to head south to Mississippi, where she came from. As a child Silas had deeply resented his mother for her relationships with men and the way she took him out of the world he had known.

Silas finds a picture of his mother and baby Larry

seven

> Picking up in 1982, this chapter recounts Larry Ott's connection to the disappearance of Cindy Walker and how those events shaped the rest of his life and the lives of his parents.

Cindy has encouraged Larry to take her out on a date. He believes they are going to the drive-in to see *The Amityville Horror*[8], but she

---

8 Horror film (1979), based on the novel by Jay Anson.

3.2 Summaries

tells him that he is to drop her off somewhere else so that she can see her secret boyfriend, and that because she is pregnant he must swear to never tell anyone about it. Larry follows her instructions, but she never appears at the arranged meeting place later that night. When he returns to the Walker's house he is attacked by Cecil Walker. Soon after, the police are summoned.

Initially, Larry tells the sheriff an abbreviated version of what happened, leaving out specific details in order to protect Cindy and himself. But when, over time, witnesses mention having seen him leaving the drive-in, he becomes the focus of greater suspicion.

Ruined family life

Eventually, Larry leaves to join the army. The suspicion and pressure put on him and his family have driven his father, who no longer speaks to him, to drink ever more heavily, and his mother has become increasingly withdrawn and depressed. While in the army he becomes a qualified mechanic. Returning to Chabot after his military service, Larry takes over his father's garage after he dies in a drunk driving accident. His mother has to be moved into a nursing home. Larry is forced to sell large parts of his family's property to the Rutherford lumber business, and he lives solely on the money from those land sales. The garage generates no income.

eight

Zombie mask

Silas meets Angie for lunch in the diner where his mother used to work. He confesses to Angie that he and Larry used to be friends and tells her his history, moving to Chabot from Chicago. He recalls an episode from their time at school together when Larry had been invited to a Halloween party because he had a cool zombie mask, but that he had been ignored by the other kids, including Silas and Cindy, and had eventually driven off alone. Silas lies to Angie about the nature of his relationship with Cindy. He later goes to the hospital to see Larry.

3.2 Summaries

Larry has undergone surgery and is still unconscious. The nurse tells him that Larry was clinically dead at two points during the operations. After visiting Larry, Silas knows that he has to also inform Larry's mother about the shooting. He goes to the nursing home, River Acres. Mrs Ott has Alzheimer's and doesn't understand who Silas is.

Silas remembers the day he spent at the Ott house when he and Larry were children. He remembers mowing the lawn, and how when Carl Ott came home that evening he had thanked Larry (whom he thought had done the work), and how angry he, Silas, had been about Larry having a father and him not having one.

He now believes that his father had been a white man who had impregnated his mother when she worked as a maid, and that his mother had left Chabot for Chicago to have her illegitimate baby.

Fatherless Silas

On the return trip to the Ott house, Silas pulls over a young white man called Wallace Stringfellow who has been driving suspiciously. But Silas is too preoccupied with thoughts of the cabin where he used to live with his mother to do more than give the man a warning and send him off.

He goes to the cabin where they used to live. He sees through a window what appears to be a fresh grave dug in the dirt floor beneath one of the beds.

nine

Larry recalls having scared away a boy who used to sneak into his barn and steal things and cause disturbances. He was 31 at the time. He put on the zombie mask he got for the Halloween party years before and ambushed the boy in the barn. Years later, aged 41, Larry is visited by a drunk young man in a TV satellite installation van who introduces himself as Wallace Stringfellow – it's the boy from ten years earlier.

Larry scares Wallace

3.2 Summaries

Wallace is a drunk and a liar, but Larry is so crippled by loneliness that he doesn't object to the visits from Wallace, and the two men become friends, Wallace visiting regularly and getting drunk and stoned on Larry's porch. One Christmas, he secretly gives Larry an old pistol as a present.

Wallace Stringfellow visits Larry

On one visit, Wallace starts to ask about whether Larry had actually raped and killed Cindy Walker, and becomes increasingly excited and sexually aroused by the idea of kidnapping, abusing and raping a girl. He has found the cabin in the woods where Silas and his mother had lived – he fantasises about this cabin having been the site of the rape and murder. He talks about how his mother's 'boyfriends' used to behave with his mother and his obvious arousal makes Larry increasingly uncomfortable. Larry tells Wallace to go home. Wallace becomes angry and smashes up Larry's car. He doesn't return to Larry's after that evening.

Despite the insights he has had into Wallace's dangerous and deviant character, Larry misses him and hopes he will come back, even to the point of considering employing him at his garage and training him to be a mechanic. His loneliness appears to hold sway over his judgement.

ten

Silas is working traffic duty one week after discovering the grave and Tina Rutherford's body in the cabin on Larry's property where he and his mother used to live. He gets a phone call from the nursing home where Larry's mother lives, informing him, as he had requested, that she is having a "good day".

Extra work for Silas

Silas has begun working extra shifts – doing guard duty over the comatose Larry in the hospital and also spending time at the Ott farm, feeding the chickens and guarding the property. He is becoming increasingly exhausted by the extra work.

3.2 Summaries

He goes to see Larry's mother at the nursing home. She vaguely remembers him and seems worried about Larry. A "stringy-looking" young white man (p. 232.30) has been spotted trying to get near Larry's room in the hospital.

At dinner, Angie forces Silas to finally tell her about his relationship with Cindy Walker back in school. They had been together secretly, but Silas' mother had found out and begged him to stop seeing her. Cecil Walker had become increasingly suspicious of Cindy and tried to control her completely. Silas had been the secret boyfriend she had wanted to meet on the night she made Larry take her to the drive-in.

Silas and Cindy Walker

Angie understands immediately what this means: Silas has known all these years that Larry was not guilty, but has said nothing and allowed Larry to take the blame and be ostracized under the suspicion of having something to do with the disappearance of Cindy Walker. Silas guesses that it was actually Cecil who killed her.

The next day, while feeding the chickens at Larry's farm, he gets a phone call from the hospital. Larry has woken from his coma.

eleven

Larry wakes up in the hospital: He has been dreaming about himself and Silas, and then himself and Wallace. French and Sheriff Lolly begin questioning him but he has a seizure when they tell him what happened to Tina Rutherford. They return another time to continue questioning him.

Both French and Lolly are convinced that Larry killed both Cindy Walker and Tina Rutherford and shot himself in a suicide attempt. They try to persuade Larry that this is what happened, disregarding his inability to remember the events or explain why he would have done these things. Larry – due to blood loss and the trauma of the

Suspicion: Larry is guilty twice

3.2 Summaries

shooting – can't remember what happened when he was shot or even if he actually did kill Tina Rutherford.

twelve

Silas is the secret boyfriend of Cindy

Silas rushes to the hospital, knowing that French will be trying to force a confession out of Larry. He defends Larry, saying he had nothing to do with the disappearance of Cindy Walker, and finally, 25 years later, confesses to having been the secret boyfriend she had made Larry take her to see. Larry and French and Lolly are shocked by the revelation. French interviews Silas back in his office, and tells him to stay away from Larry from now on.

Later, Silas is getting drunk in a bar when Irina (the woman with the rattlesnake in her mailbox) comes in and starts drinking with him. She tells him about a friend of hers, Evelyn, who had been seeing a weird young white guy who collected guns and snakes. His name was Wallace Stringfellow. Irina thinks he may have been the person who put snakes in her and Evelyn's mailbox. Silas vaguely remembers the name and the man. He goes home with Irina, but has second thoughts and leaves before anything can happen between them.

thirteen

Larry is in hospital still, watching TV. He is remembering scenes and moments from his childhood, with Silas and with Cindy, in a confused jumble which stirs his emotions.

Larry remembers

He also now remembers how, shortly after Tina Rutherford went missing, Wallace came to his place, waking him at 3:15 in the morning. He was drunk, sitting outside on the porch. He half-confessed to having done "something", and seemed depressed and full of self-hatred. When Larry offered to teach him how to fix cars, Wallace replied that he wasn't "worth a shit".

3.2 Summaries

Larry wants to tell French what he has remembered, and that he is sure it was Wallace who killed Tina and shot him.

fourteen

Silas goes to work the next morning with a bad hangover. He later goes back to Larry's farm to feed the chickens. There he sees fresh tire tracks from the 4-wheel vehicle he had noticed there before and an empty can of Pabst Blue Ribbon beer. He begins to think about Wallace, and decides to go and talk to him about the snakes that had been put in Irina's mailbox.

He goes to Wallace's house and interviews him. He sees John Wayne Gacy, Wallace's vicious and mistreated pitbull-Chow cross-breed dog, he sees the snakes, and then also spots Larry's old zombie mask, from the Halloween party 25 years ago. When Silas asks him about it, Wallace makes an excuse to go outside and then releases the dog. The dog immediately attacks Silas, biting and wounding him before he can defend himself or get to his radio. While Silas is fighting off the dog, Wallace begins shooting at him. Silas manages to get his own gun and shoots the dog.

Silas gets injured in Wallace's house

Silas then shoots Wallace in the leg, but Wallace escapes into a nearby wood. Silas is badly injured and collapses in Wallace's house, smashing one of the snake enclosures and releasing a rattlesnake as he falls. The last thing he sees is Larry's zombie mask.

fifteen

Larry hears from the deputy guarding his hospital room that Silas has been hurt and figures out that it has to do with Wallace. He tells the deputy that he has to talk to French about Wallace.

Over the deputy's radio, he describes to French what he remembers of Wallace and his disturbing ideas, the last time he visited

1 FORWORD –
AT A GLANCE

2 TOM FRANKLIN:
LIFE & WORK

3 ANALYSES AND
INTERPRETATIONS

3.2   Summaries

Wallace placed
a diamondback
rattlesnake in
Irina's mailbox
© picture alliance /
PIXSELL

him, and that he recognised Wallace's eyes behind the mask when
he was shot. He describes the mask to French.

French later comes to Larry's room and has him identify the mask.
He asks Larry some questions about Wallace and their relationship,
and then informs Larry that Wallace is now dead.

Later, after French has left, Larry is thinking about time passing
and loneliness and memories when he gets a new roommate: Silas
is brought in.

3.2 Summaries

sixteen

Silas wakes up in the hospital room next to Larry – his brother, both of them the sons of Carl Ott – and remembers what happened and how he got here. The TV is on and they watch a news report about the events at Wallace's house. Silas learns from the report that after he passed out in Wallace's house, his colleague Voncille notified the sheriff's department, and there was a gun battle during which Wallace allegedly shot and killed himself. When the officers searched Wallace's house they found evidence that implicated him in the murder of Tina Rutherford, including her purse.

Silas tells Larry everything he has learned, including that they are half-brothers. Larry says that he thinks he already knew back when they first met, and after the incident with the coats. When Silas finishes talking, Larry summons the nurse and tells her he wants to be moved to another room.

Silas and Larry are half-brothers

seventeen

Silas has lots of visitors on the next day, his last day in hospital. Angie, Voncille and the mayor all come to see him. Then French comes to inform them both about the progress with the case against Wallace. They now know that he shot Larry and killed Tina. They also believe that he may have been responsible for the murder of M&M, too. He cautions them both to be careful when facing journalists, because the case has attracted nationwide attention and there are TV crews at the hospital from CNN and Fox News, as well as from local stations.

Wallace is the culprit

eighteen

Angie drives Silas home from the hospital. He drops in at City Hall where the mayor tells him he will be getting a new car and some assistance in his work, apparently to be financed by Tina Ruther-

3.2 Summaries

ford's father. Silas tells the mayor to wait until he sees the story coming out in the local paper before he authorises any of this.

Larry refuses to talk to Silas

He then goes home to convalesce. He visits Larry, who refuses to talk to him. He also goes to visit Mrs Ott in the nursing home, but she doesn't know who he is, lost in dementia. He goes to look at the derelict Walker house.

nineteen

Four days later: Silas has visited Larry every day, but while he enjoys the visits, Larry doesn't know how to react or what to say. Silas has been taking care of things for him, feeding the chickens, bringing him his mail and his cheque book so he can pay his bills.

Larry dismisses himself from hospital

The doctor tells Larry he can start moving around now, but that he must start eating a healthier diet. Larry takes short walks around the hospital, noticing all the reporters outside waiting for him. Late that night he sneaks out of the hospital. He starts to walk home.

Silas gets a phone call from the hospital telling him that Larry has left, and he immediately gets in his car and heads off to find him. He discovers Larry walking home. Silas drives him home, and Larry offers to fix up Silas' jeep.

Larry forgives Silas

Larry is surprised that Silas and Angie have cleaned up his house while he was in hospital. Larry says Silas should come by the next day so they can work on the Jeep. Their friendship appears to be restored.

3.3 Structure

SUMMARY

Crooked Letter, Crooked Letter is structured as a crime thriller: a crime occurs early in the narrative and the plot involves solving the crime. The novel is also concerned with events in the past, and so it is structured to include long passages of flashbacks to 25 years ago. Other structural elements which organise the plot and the characters include the use of symmetry to highlight both divisions and similarities. Here we will also look at the evolution of the friendship between Larry and Wallace as an organising structure in the novel.

The title

The concept of place – the idea of where you are, where you belong – and the actual physical location are important in the novel. Alice and Silas' transition from the northern city of Chicago (the third largest city in the USA) to this tiny hamlet in **rural Mississippi** is a big deal: For the 13-year old Silas it's a completely different world. The racial and social tensions and dynamics of rural Mississippi are not the same as in Chicago, a major northern city. And for Larry Ott, his notoriety as "Scary Larry" is greatly exacerbated by his location in a **tiny community** where everyone knows everyone else – a community he has never really left, with the exception of his short time in the military.

This idea of the **central importance of place** in the novel begins with the title. Taken from a children's rhyme used as a mnemonic for the correct spelling of Mississippi (the crooked letter meaning the letter "s"), the title *Crooked Letter* immediately and firmly anchors the novel and our expectations in a specific place,

Crooked Letter "s"

3.3 Structure

namely the deep South, and gives it a specific frame of reference: **Childhood**.

The idea of belonging

The idea of belonging is a **central theme in the novel**, and the characters belong to this specific place in varying degrees. We have Larry, who has never left and is tied to a place where he is now a pariah, and Silas, who was conceived here, but who grew up far to the north before being brought back as a teenager, only to leave again, and return yet again as an adult. Alice's inability to successfully leave this specific place behind her is an important device within the plot of the novel, a device which is used to bring Silas into the story, and to expose the secrets within Carl Ott's past. The place, **Chabot in Mississippi**, won't let people go: Larry can't escape. Alice can't escape. And Silas is dragged back twice, also unable to escape.

Chronology

The novel is concerned with the connected events of **two different times** – the year 1982 and the present day (presumably 2007, 25 years later). The narrative makes strong use of flashbacks, at times with entire chapters being set in the past (Chapters 3, 5 and 7) but also in shorter forms, with the central characters Larry and Silas **remembering moments** from their past and the events which drove them apart.

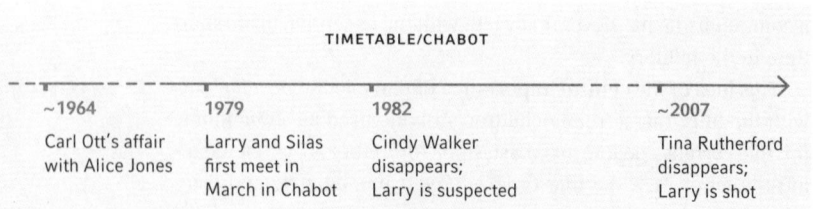

TIMETABLE/CHABOT

~1964	1979	1982	~2007
Carl Ott's affair with Alice Jones	Larry and Silas first meet in March in Chabot	Cindy Walker disappears; Larry is suspected	Tina Rutherford disappears; Larry is shot

3.3 Structure

The extensive use of flashbacks means that the structure of the novel must be considered in two different ways. Firstly, there is the surface structure, the sequence of chapters and narrative, which moves back and forth in time and follows the demands of the plot and the creation and release of tension and suspense. Then there is **the internal chronology**, the actual sequence of events within the lives of the characters in the novel, beginning with the first meeting between Larry and Silas in March 1979. (There is of course another, older part of the story – the affair between Alice Jones and Carl Ott – which is only reconstructed after both have died, and which can be understood by the reader as a kind of lost or hidden prologue to the story.)

Flashbacks

The frequent use of flashbacks not only means that the novel has two structures: It also means that events in the past are looked at from two perspectives, those of **childhood and adulthood**. Major events – such as Silas's first and only visit to Larry's home when they were boys – are approached carefully, in stages. When Silas goes to investigate the Ott farm after Larry's shooting (pp. 85–95) there are brief mentions of his having been there before, and a lengthier description (pp. 87.20–88.10) of Silas' recollections of that day. This event is seen later, in greater detail and with more emotional reflection, from the boys' perspectives.

Childhood and adulthood

We see events from one chronological perspective – adult or child – and then from another. This is significant, because many of the greatest conflicts in the novel – in particular the guilt Larry feels for having called Silas "n****r" and the guilt Silas feels for having betrayed Larry by not speaking up about Cindy Walker – are **hidden in the past**, but have enormous consequences throughout the two men's lives. One target the novel moves towards is the possible reconciliation between Larry and Silas, which requires both of them to re-evaluate events from 25 years ago, to reflect on the feelings

The past influences the characters

3.3 Structure

and impressions from the time and to consider their changed circumstances and the **different perspectives** they now have as adults.

An example of how the two time frames interact

As an example of how the two time frames interact, we can look at the end of Chapter 4, the content of Chapter 5 and the beginning of Chapter 6. Chapter 4 is set in the present day and ends with Silas in his own home, having returned from investigating the crime scene at Larry's home. Two things are important here at the end of the chapter. Most obviously significant is the message from Larry on Silas' answer machine, a phone call made before he was shot. The second is less explicit but equally important: "In the closet, behind his two extra uniforms, where he wouldn't have to look at it, was the Marlin lever-action .22 rifle." (p. 96.21–23)

The symbol of the rifle

The chapter which follows is about the significance of this small detail. It describes the events leading up to the scene where Carl Ott forces Larry and Silas to **fight for possession of the gun**, the .22 Marlin. While it is Silas' memory which is triggered in the present, we see this episode from the past from Larry's perspective. The scene is of **central importance** for the entire book and for many of the themes – brothers, fathers and friends; guilt; race – and it is the single most important event in the course of Larry and Silas' relationship. The chapter from the past is therefore introduced and given context by a guilty memory of Silas' in the present day. This detour into the past is touched on again at the beginning of the next chapter when Silas acknowledges to himself that he used the event – Larry calling him "n****r" – as an excuse to avoid him (p. 121.11–13). The rifle also makes another appearance (p. 125.8–10). What we as readers don't know yet is that this **level of guilt and anger** covers a much deeper and much more damaging guilt – Silas' guilt at never

3.3 Structure

having spoken up to save Larry from the suspicions surrounding Cindy Walker's disappearance.

Symmetries

A fundamental **organisational structure** of the novel involves contrasting symmetries. This can be seen most significantly in the mirrored events of 1982 and the present day – the disappearances of local girls – and in the two central characters, brothers who are diametric opposites.

Events and characters

There are numerous other examples of symmetries throughout the book. One significant example is the way that Larry and Wallace both wear the **zombie mask** to scare one another. Larry uses it to frighten young Wallace when he is trespassing (pp. 195–6) and Wallace wears it when he ambushes and shoots Larry (p. 23).

The zombie mask

LARRY	SILAS
White	Black
Shy and lonely	Gregarious and popular
Avid reader	Not a reader
Neither talented at or interested in sports	Gifted athlete, especially baseball
Single	In a relationship
Teetotal	Likes to drink
Country boy, knowledge of nature	City kid, knows nothing about wildlife
Raised by both parents	Single mother, father unknown
"Where Larry's only visitors had been law enforcement officials …	… Silas had a stream." (306.1–2)

As the two characters who flank Larry, Silas and Wallace are also related in a contrasting symmetry. Both are Larry's friends. One

Larry's two friends

3.3 Structure

white, one black, one a half-brother, the other a strange kind of symbolic shadow **brother, Wallace and Silas** embody the themes and ideas of the novel in their oppositional symmetry.

SILAS	WALLACE
Black	White
Gregarious and popular	Creepy and disliked
Single mother, father unknown	Single mother, father unknown
Destroys Larry's life by concealing the truth about the night Cindy Walker disappeared.	Destroys Larry's life by framing him for the murder of Tina Rutherford and shooting him.
Returns often to Larry's home after the shooting – to investigate and to keep an eye on the place	Keeps returning to Larry's home after having shot him (see 289.5–16)

Missing girls

The two missing girls, **Cindy and Tina**, also embody certain themes and ideas within the novel.

CINDY WALKER	TINA RUTHERFORD
Disappears, presumed murdered.	Disappears, presumed murdered.
Body never found – presumed murdered, but the killer is never officially identified.	Body discovered and murderer identified and killed.
Poor, considered "white trash". Wants to leave school with Silas.	Privileged daughter of the region's most prominent and wealthy family. Attends university.
Fully characterised in the novel. We meet her, see her interact with different characters and hear her speak. As a character, Cindy is as real to the reader as Silas or Larry.	Nothing but a name and a corpse. We never meet Tina nor ever hear her voice. She is missing and presumed dead from the beginning. Despite being the central focus of the crime thriller-plot of the novel (see the opening sentence) Tina is never "real" as a character.

3.3 Structure

Two central characters

Larry and Silas are the central characters of the novel. They both tell the story from their own perspective, narrating the past as well as the present. While Larry is the central figure in the novel, Silas is the more active agent: He investigates the crimes, he becomes increasingly drawn into Larry's world, and, as the plot unfolds, we learn that he is also deeply involved in the issue of how Larry became what and who he is in the present. What also emerges is that these two central characters are in fact brothers.

Brothers

The majority of the present day level of the novel is told from **Silas' perspective**, not least because Larry spends most of the period in question – roughly two weeks from the shooting to the end of the novel – in a coma. In contrast, Chapters 5 and 7, describing the friendship between the boys and the fight over the gun (5) and the events surrounding the disappearance of Cindy Walker (7) are told from **Larry's perspective**. This is significant because it reinforces the impression we have of Larry as someone who is a **prisoner of the past**, someone who has been unable to break away from those events and who has been defined by them. Silas is a more **active agent** in the present day: He investigates, he interacts with people, he moves around. Larry is literally frozen in time – in a coma – for most of the present day narrative of the novel.

Perspectives

Suspense and foreshadowing

Because the novel is in essence a **crime thriller** about the connected mysteries of who killed Tina Rutherford and who shot Larry Ott, as well as what happened to Cindy Walker 25 years ago, the narrative requires suspense. Suspense is created here by the author withholding information, revealing facts and details to the reader through the actions and thoughts of the characters. The primary agent of this investigation into the details of what has happened is

Crime fiction techniques

3.3 Structure

Silas, who is a police constable. A major tool used by the author to create suspense and a sense of mystery is the use of flashbacks in combination with cryptic thoughts and **memories** of the characters as adults.

There are individual moments of shock, suspense and the use of foreshadowing, as should be expected from a crime thriller. Examples include:

The monster

→ **Larry being shot (pp. 17–25)**

From the opening sentence of the novel, we know that a monster is coming. We aren't shown it immediately: The narrative draws back and shows us Larry and his morning routines. There are details about how he cares for the chickens, this strange lonely man pottering around in his house as he gets ready to go to work. The tone is **calm and contemplative**. After a while we probably, as readers, are no longer wondering consciously about the missing girl and the monster waiting for him.

When Larry returns home after having received the call from the nursing home, he is ambushed by the intruder in his house. This is the monster. Wearing a **zombie mask**, the intruder shoots Larry and tells him, "Die" (p. 25).

Suspense

The opening sequence uses a technique of suspense-building which involves luring the reader into a **false sense of security**. We are warned in the opening sentence, then distracted by the meandering description of Larry's morning routines, and then the trap springs shut.

→ **Silas in the barn (p. 88)**

The jump scare

This is an example of what in cinematic terms is called a "jump scare": A sudden shock creates a fright and/or shock with its speed and suddenness. Typically a jump scare will turn out to be something

3.3   Structure

which is not dangerous. The characters (and the audience) have been conditioned by the narrative to be alert, to **expect danger** of some kind. This tension and expectant alertness means that the trigger – the jump scare itself – can create a much **more intense and explosive scare effect** than the situation or the event itself would normally have been able to.

In this example we have Silas investigating Larry's farm and property. We know that a violent crime was committed here, and Silas is in this precise moment concerned about **snakes in the barn**. His heightened sense of danger and alertness means that the jump scare, when it comes – the chickens – triggers his reactions. He "yelped" and fires his gun in **shocked reaction**.

→ Foreshadowing Wallace Stringfellow (p. 92.8–9)

Silas and Roy French, searching Larry's house, discover the DIRECTV brochures left by Wallace. The significance is not clear to us as readers – we haven't yet seen Wallace pretending to be a DIRECTV salesman when he first comes to visit Larry – or to Silas or French. But it is a clue, a detail that holds the fabric of a narrative together which is based around the rules of the crime fiction genre. There has to be logic, a progression of events and revealing of information which **the reader can follow** or retrace without feeling cheated.

Detailed information

→ The mask as a clue (p. 293)

This is a more explicit clue than the example above. In this scene Silas is in Wallace's house, he sees Larry's zombie mask, and knows for sure that it was Wallace who had shot Larry. The mask has been present from the beginning of the book and is already charged with a rich **variety of meanings** for us as readers, as well as for the characters. Silas knows the mask: It was worn by Larry to the Halloween

The zombie mask

party where he, Silas, made a conscious decision to finally turn his back on his former friend. We as readers know that Wallace wore the mask to shoot Larry. We also know that Larry wore the mask to scare young Wallace. The presence of the mask here, the shockingly realistic and gory zombie head, highlights the crisis. On the level of crime fiction genre techniques, the mask infuses this scene with a sense of events having come full circle, which will always imply a crisis, and it provides Silas, our investigator, with **the last piece of the puzzle**.

→ Wallace lurking in the hospital (pp. 232–234)

Advantage of the readers

As readers of *Crooked Letter* we experience the plot differently from the characters. We know things about the past which Larry and Silas can't know, and **we know more** about Larry's life, specifically his contact with Wallace, than Silas could possibly know. So when Silas sees a shadowy, stringy-looking form in the distance in the hospital and feels slightly unnerved by it, we know that he (and particularly the helpless and comatose Larry) has good reason to be afraid. We know that this is Wallace, lurking around the hospital, maybe hoping for a chance to finish Larry off. The sense of dread is heightened for us and we can feel anxiety as well for our investigator – Silas doesn't know who or what is lurking in the distance. His **lack of knowledge** makes him vulnerable, and his vulnerability raises the tension for us as well.

Suspense and tension

This is a necessary **technique for crime fiction** (as well as for many other fiction formats) because the bottom line is creating suspense and tension, and a character with perfect knowledge who is never in any danger would be incapable of providing either. In order for crime fiction to work, the protagonists have to work with **limited information** and, figuratively speaking, to grope in the dark, not fully aware of the nature of the threat they face.

3.3 Structure

As a footnote to this, and in reference to the **film** *Silence of the Lambs* (which is discussed in the section on Horror in Chapter 3.5 – Notes on Themes), one of the most famous examples of this particular technique involves the heroine of the film, FBI agent Clarice Starling, groping blindly in a completely dark cellar while the killer stalks her wearing night-vision goggles. This famous scene is a perfect display of this fundamental and necessary technique in suspense fiction.

Silence of the Lambs (1988): novel by Thomas Harris

→ **Silas sends Angie to Larry's farm on a hunch (pp. 47, 82–83)**
Good police work always involves hunches. An investigator's **instincts** are every bit as valuable as his or her trained skills. French comments on this ("You after my job?") because of course he can see that this was a very good move by the relatively inexperienced police constable. Had Silas not thought of sending Angie to Larry's place, then Larry would have died and the truth – that Wallace killed Tina and shot Larry and that Larry had nothing to do with the deaths of either Cindy or Tina – would never have come out.

Hunches are intuitive leaps, and as readers we also make **intuitive leaps** through the plots of what we read. We are guided by the information given to us by the author, but are also expected to make certain leaps by ourselves – this is particularly true of crime fiction, where we are trained to a certain extent by genre expectations to **identify certain patterns** and draw conclusions, anticipating the resolution provided by the author.

The role of the reader

→ **Foreshadowing the relationship between Silas and Larry**
Crime fiction relies heavily on the building up of suspense, but also on the laying out of clues for the reader, foreshadowing revelations or hinting at secrets and motivations. *Crooked Letter* works with these techniques. For example, very early on in the novel, during

Logical plot

3.3   Structure

the first flashback chapter (pp. 56–81) we have Larry's memories of having first encountered Alice and Silas Jones. Carl Ott asks Alice to introduce the two boys to one another: "'Larry,' the woman said, as if she knew him." (p. 57.9) What Larry will not learn for another 25 years until after he has woken from his coma and heard the truth from Silas, is that Alice of course *does* know him: She was his nanny. This will not be revealed to us as readers until Silas finds the photos in Larry's attic (p. 130.12–29). His discovery is later confirmed by Ina Ott on one of her good days in the nursing home (pp. 237–239). But the **seeds of the truth** have been planted early on in the book; when the revelation comes, we as readers will not feel cheated – that the author has produced some shocking surprise out of nowhere, betraying our trust in him to tell us a story with care and coherence – because **the clues** were there from the beginning. The truth about Carl Ott being Silas' father is prepared in a similar way, as is the issue of Silas' guilty secret.

→ Reverse-foreshadowing the zombie mask

Symbol of murderous intent

Also of interest here is the almost reverse-foreshadowing we have with the zombie mask. We first see it in its most extreme appearance – Wallace wears it when he shoots Larry. It is only as the novel progresses that the mask is explained and we can learn where it came from and what role it has played in Larry's life up until this point. The mask is discussed in detail elsewhere in this book (see Chapter 3.5 Notes on Themes, Horror and monsters) but it is significant in this context of crime fiction techniques for its recurring role and the way it is used to constantly **remind us of the crime** we see at the opening of the novel – Larry being shot. It makes its last major appearance in the showdown between Silas and Wallace. Silas sees it, recognises it, and both he and Wallace in that moment know that the game is up. Its significance as a symbol and a clue has

3.3 Structure

In *Crooked Letter* the mask is a very special symbol.
© picture alliance / Wolfram Steinberg

been carefully laid out throughout the novel, and while **its meaning changes** – it's a source of delight for young Larry but a symbol of murderous intent by the end – it represents a very effective use of traditional literary techniques from the genre of crime fiction.

Crime fiction and collateral damage

The disappearances of Cindy Walker and Tina Rutherford are the pivotal events in the novel, but they are not what the novel itself is most interested in: The focus is very much on the **collateral damage** of the two crimes. While Roy French is investigating the mechanics

3.3 Structure

of the crimes (including the shooting of Larry Ott) Silas Jones is diving deeper into his own history and his entanglement with Larry. And while Larry is in a coma, his role as **"Scary Larry"** is being embraced from opposite directions by both Wallace Stringfellow and Roy French, while at the same time Silas is working to deconstruct the myth of Larry as a killer.

Friendship and betrayel

The novel is more concerned with this relationship and the dynamics of friendship and betrayal than it is with the crimes. The murder of Tina Rutherford and the character of Wallace are almost like the symbolic offspring of "Scary Larry". Something which was never true – that Larry killed Cindy – has become the **inspiration and obsession for Wallace** to make real his twisted fantasies. Despite being the focus of this obsession, Larry is innocent. He did nothing wrong. Indirectly, the blame lies with Silas: His silence concerning the true events of that night in 1982 could have saved Larry from becoming "Scary Larry" and could have denied Wallace a focus for his dangerous obsession.

"Scary Larry"

A passage describing the events following the night of Cindy's disappearance up until the present day is particularly interesting (pp. 170–173). The police procedural aspects of the story, the classic structures of crime fiction – the search for Cindy, the questioning of suspects, the canvassing of witnesses and the hunt for evidence – are described in a dazed rush, blended with the equally stunned and rapid decay of the Ott family, as Larry becomes completely isolated, Carl becomes a serious alcoholic and his business begins to fail, and Ina's mental state breaks down. **The family is completely broken**: "Their lives had stopped, frozen" (171.12).

Larry: Suspicious and guilty

But it is still a crime novel, and key elements in the plot involve standard techniques of the genre. The demands of suspense in a crime novel or thriller dictate that there must be **mystery about who did what to whom**, as well as when, why and how. Larry's

3.3 Structure

situation becomes much, much worse when the police catch him in a lie (p. 170.7–8) and he immediately appears more suspicious and guilty than he actually is. Silas' silence makes his terrible position even worse. From the perspective of the investigators in 1982, and later, in the present day, from the perspective of Roy French and Sheriff Lolly, Larry is too convenient a suspect to ignore. Everything about him signals guilt. French and Lolly try to pressure Larry into confessing: It seems that this is not just laziness on their part – having a convenient suspect helpless in a hospital, easy to coerce – but French seems to be genuinely convinced that Larry is responsible. **Larry's only hope for rescue lies with Silas**.

Silas not only knows the truth of what happened in 1982, and can eventually exonerate Larry from all suspicion of having killed Cindy Walker – he is also the only person in the present day who is trying to prove that Larry is not guilty of having killed Tina Rutherford. He returns again and again to **Larry's home**, both to investigate and search for any clues he might have missed, as well as to care for the chickens and keep an eye on the place out of guilt-inspired loyalty. It is while investigating yet again (pp. 288–289) and after having learned from Irina about her friend Evelyn's connection with Wallace Stringfellow, that he sees clear signs that Wallace has been hanging around Larry's house.

Silas investigates

Silas' activities combine the demands of crime fiction – an investigator searching for clues – with the emotional, personal level of the story – the collateral damage.

Cindy as focus

Larry's problems really and truly begin with the **disappearance of Cindy Walker**. From this point onwards, his life is basically ruined. Her disappearance also provides, years later, the inspiration for Wallace Stringfellow to act on his disturbing fantasies. If that

Initial event: night of 1982

3.3 Structure

evening in 1982 had not happened, Larry would not have dropped out of school and become "Scary Larry". Cindy's death functions as an initial event – an original Big Bang – from which the plot of the novel develops.

Fatal triangle

Cindy was extremely important for both **Larry and Silas**, albeit in different ways: Silas enjoyed her as a girlfriend, but he was unable or unwilling to take her seriously as a person. His coldness at the end of their time together holds her at bay. Larry was infatuated with her, and used to spy on her from a distance. When Silas jumps up to confront Cecil and Carl when they are pestering her, Larry remains in hiding. Silas finally pushes her away when she becomes too needy – and Larry is destroyed by her betrayal of his availability and infatuation.

The evolution of the friendship: Larry and Wallace

Two friends of Larry: Silas and Wallace

Larry has two friendships: with Silas and with Wallace. The relationship with Silas forms the larger structure and the story at the heart of *Crooked Letter*, beginning in the past and developing until it reaches its conclusion in Silas's confession and Larry's forgiveness. The **relationship between Larry and Wallace** covers less time and takes up less space in the novel, but it is this relationship which contains the true plot of the novel – the murder of Tina and the shooting of Larry – and provides in a sense the machinery which powers the book in its function as a crime thriller.

Outsiders Larry and Wallace: "losers"

Larry's friendship with Wallace begins with a lie and a deception – Wallace claiming to be a DIRECTV salesman and pretending that he doesn't know who Larry is (pp. 197 ff.). But underneath this, the two outsiders do have some **common ground**. Friendship requires shared experiences, interests, attitudes, complementary temperaments – something, anything shared, something that establishes common ground. Despite Wallace obviously being what

3.3 Structure

is usually referred to as "white trash" (see section below on Class and Status for more on the term) and Larry coming from a land-owning family (his father owned over 500 acres of land before Larry started selling to the Rutherfords), neither of them finished high school (p. 201.6–16). This is something they have in common which arises very early in their first conversation. It is a sign of their **outsider status**, something which brands them both as **"losers"** in modern society. It should also be noted that Wallace, being a white racist who is delighted that his vicious dog immediately attacks black people, would never have approached Larry had he not been white. Race here provides a very basic common ground for Wallace to build a relationship upon.

There is more to the **solidarity of outsiders**, something Wallace addresses when he tells Larry the story of how he first saw him in the church (pp. 211–213). He says that other boys who attended the same service and had seen Larry there wanted to warn him to never come back to their church. Larry expresses understanding: "You can't blame them." Wallace says "Naw. But fuck em anyway." (p. 213.13–14) Wallace here expresses a kinship with Larry. He defiantly rejects society for its rejection of Larry and himself. Larry felt something of this, too: When he is planning to tell Roy French about Wallace and his suspicions, he thinks that, remembering Wallace as a boy, that he "saw a little of himself in him, maybe. This disastrous triangle. Maybe, to this kid, in this world Larry hadn't caught up to, Larry was even a kind of hero." (p. 284.5–8)

"Strange lonely kid"

After **Wallace's first visit** (as an adult) to Larry's place, Larry lies in bed that night and "smiled in the dark" (p. 202.23–24). He recognised Wallace as the boy from ten years ago and knows he was being lied to. But the human interaction, the presence of someone who is interested in him, wants to talk to him – the prospect of friendship – is more important to him. He is "disappointed but not

Human interaction

3.3 Structure

surprised" when Wallace doesn't return the next Monday, as he said he would (p. 203.6–13).

Wallace returns two months later (from p. 203). Their friendship begins here. Larry responds to being teased about his introverted nature with a kind of delight (pp. 204.30–205.7) and Wallace's concern about Larry not having a **gun** to protect himself and his property from aggressive trespassers certainly appears to be genuine (p. 205.29–206.2). He later gives Larry a gun as a present (pp. 214–215): the same gun with which he eventually shoots him.

As Wallace begins to open up and talk more – he talks constantly and doesn't seem to need much in the way of a response from Larry – he talks about how he first heard of Larry (pp. 210–214). There is an element of awe and hero-worship in the way Wallace talks about Larry (remember that Wallace's idea of Scary Larry – the terrifying murderer – has nothing to do with the truth). He talks about fishing in "the same water you did" (p. 210.29, a highly symbolic statement) and he clearly remembers **every detail** of what teachers at school said about Larry when he had been a student there (p. 211.14–18). The first time he ever saw Larry in the flesh is also firmly fixed in his memory (p. 211.19–213.14), when Larry came to a church service Wallace and his mother were attending. We get a sense that Wallace feels he was in the presence of a living legend – later, we learn more about Wallace's fascination with rape and murder. But here, in the early days of their friendship, we already have the slightly alarming impression of a teenage boy who is hero-worshipping a man he believed to have murdered a young girl: "I watched you the whole time" (p. 212.23). Larry remembers having seen the boy there: Wallace runs out of the church. Larry remembers the "boy who followed him out, called 'Hey' in a way he'd not heard before, not angry but curious" (p. 213.2–3). The close attention of the almost star-struck Wallace made Larry feel very uncomfortable at the time.

3.3 Structure

For Larry, Wallace is only **the second friend** he has ever had. The other one was Silas. He at one point draws a direct comparison between them by observing their different reactions to the same story: At New Year, he and Silas fire off rockets and Larry is reminded of the night with the Walkers when **Cecil set himself on fire**. He had told Silas the story, and Silas had not found it funny. "But now as Larry told it Wallace began to laugh as Larry imitated Cecil running and pounding his pocket" (p. 216.17–21). This is a rare **direct comparison** made by Larry between the only two friends he ever had, both of whom, it should be remembered, were at the time outsiders. He was never supposed to have contact with and certainly not be friends with Silas, who was poor and black, and Wallace is the lowest kind of rural degenerate. The difference in their reactions which Larry notices highlights for us as readers the difference in character between Silas and Wallace. Silas has more empathy. He is only too aware of the callousness the story exposes, Cecil's idiocy and the cruelty behind the laughter at his stupid, dangerous behaviour. But Wallace, like Larry a country-bred boy, has a robust, rough sense of humour (he exhibits his sense of humour often and enjoys Larry's dry humour) and shares the Otts' and the Walkers' ability to laugh at the slapstick consequences of **stupid actions**. This highlights again a shared sense of belonging here between Larry and Wallace: They come from the same general **background and environment**, despite their differences in status and upbringing. Silas, the boy from the northern city, is in this situation an outsider, unimpressed by the rough and cruel humour.

Wallace

This small incident and comparison highlights the ambiguity of much of the novel's themes. It is not made clear to us how Larry feels about this difference between Silas and Wallace, and we as readers are also not given clear directions on how we are supposed to process the information. **It is ambiguous**. Is Silas a "better person"

Silas and Wallace

3.3 Structure

for not having laughed at such a silly story? Is Wallace closer to Larry than Silas was because he was on the same wavelength, because he got the humour of the story? Despite being Larry's half-brother, is Silas actually the outsider in this strange three-cornered relationship at the heart of the novel, Silas-Larry-Wallace, where all three of them hurt and wound one another?

Friends should accept each other as they are

Wallace explicitly invokes their friendship on the last night they spend as friends. "I don't care if you done it or not, took that girl. We'd still be friends. […] We friends, and a friend, a best friend, he wouldn't never do you that way, wouldn't never call the law on his friend, no matter what his friend done." (pp. 218.31–219.3) There are a couple of points to be made here. One, it is clear that by this point the two men, Wallace and Larry, **really are friends**, almost certainly the only friend either one has. This remains true despite whatever darkness is inside Wallace. But the second point is that Wallace's invocation of friendship here is very self-serving: He says that yes, if Larry had indeed killed Cindy, he, Wallace, would have stood by him – because they are friends. But what he means is that Larry, as his friend, should also accept him now for what he is about to say, as he abruptly lays bare his grimmest fantasies of sexual violence aimed at women, his obsession with abduction and rape, exposing his need to degrade and punish women. Despite being drunk and stoned, he is careful to remind Larry that they are friends before coming out with this.

Larry: need for friendship and social interaction

After this incident, Larry is still waiting for his friend Wallace to return. He even **imagines giving Wallace a job** (p. 222.21–27) to help keep him out of trouble. Larry's natural empathy and, again, his desperate need for friendship, let him imagine this unreal scenario in which Wallace can be "tamed" and they can live happily ever after as friends. This fantasy is in its own way every bit as unreal as Wallace's childhood fantasy of being abducted and "owned" by

3.3 Structure

Scary Larry. When Wallace visits him after having "done something" (killing Tina Rutherford, p. 282.6), Larry actually offers to take him on as an apprentice. Wallace turns him down: "'I don't believe it'd work out, Larry.' [...] 'Cause I ain't worth a shit.'" (p. 283.8–10) Larry only realises the enormous significance of this visit and conversation in hindsight: He then understands that Wallace had been struggling with the aftermath of killing Tina Rutherford, and had come to see **the only person he considered to be his friend**. In that moment Wallace is obviously feeling the burden of his crime.

3.4 Characters: Constellations & Characteristics

SUMMARY

The main characters in the novel are Larry Ott and Silas Jones. They are connected by their friendship as boys and by Carl Ott. Their parents are also important in the novel, as are individuals like Cindy Walker and Wallace Stringfellow, but the novel is essentially about these two men and their complicated and unhappy relationship.

Larry Ott

Larry is, at the time of the novel, 41 years old. The **only child of Carl and Ina Ott**, Larry was born in Chabot, where he has lived all his life, apart from the time he spent serving in the US military. Larry is average sized and is not particularly athletic. He "had been chubby as a kid" (p. 20.17) and tended towards "pudginess" (p. 61.29), but is now much leaner. He has "olive skin and straight brown hair and brown eyes with long lashes" (p. 62.32–33). As a child he was sickly and asthmatic (p. 61.26).

Disappointment to his father

His father **Carl was a domineering** and abusive presence in his life, and Larry was made to understand throughout his life that he was a huge disappointment to his father – "He understood that Carl liked most everyone except him." (61.25) His mother loved him and prayed together with him as a child.

Ott property: cabin

He lives on the Ott family property, a house with a barn and originally over 500 acres of land, including woodland in which the little cabin stands where the Jones family live and where Tina Rutherford's body is later found. Since returning from the military and the death of his father, Larry has been forced to sell areas of the Ott family property to the Rutherford timber company.

3.4 Characters: Constellations & Characteristics

Larry quit high school and volunteered for military service. He afterwards went on to work at **Ottomotive Repair**, the garage set up by his father. Although as a boy he showed no aptitude for cars, mechanics or the business of working in a garage, he learned the trade while he was serving in the military. The notoriety attached to him as "Scary Larry" (pp.43–47) has meant that the garage now has no local customers. The only business he has is from the occasional driver passing through who needs some minor work done on their car. Larry has literally no income other than the money he can get from selling his family's land. His life is a cycle of routines, (Chapter 1; p. 197) and having no real work and no social interactions, there is nothing to change the course of his days.

Boring routine

Larry is a **voracious reader** (pp. 86.21–29, 124.14–16: "Of course, he thought. Books. They were everywhere"). He is a great fan in particular of the famous horror writer **Stephen King**, some of whose books feature prominently in the novel. He never drinks alcohol (his father died in a drunk driving accident) and doesn't do drugs.

Horror fiction

As a child, Larry was different from many of his classmates: He was **shy, sensitive and more interested in nature and his books** than in sports, for which he showed no talent. His shyness is very pronounced: When he smiles he automatically covers his mouth with his hand to conceal the expression (p. 264.1–4).

Larry is terrified of black kids, but when a reorganisation of the local school districts means that he has to change schools, leaving the Fulsom school for the school in Chabot, where the student population is roughly 80% black, we see that he is more likely to feel empathy than the other white children around him. When pressured into conforming to prevalent **racist behaviour**, Larry is deeply uncomfortable and feels guilty.

Empathic

3.4 Characters: Constellations & Characteristics

This guilt comes from the fact that Larry is by nature empathetic, considerate and generous. This is evident in, for example, the efforts he makes to ensure that his mother's chickens have as comfortable a life as possible (pp. 18–19), and in his non-judgemental reaction to the deeply weird Wallace Stringfellow. As a child, he carried a gun and enjoyed hunting, but felt guilty about shooting animals (p. 68.1–4).

Religious

Larry is also quite religious. He talks about how his mother had to go to a different church after the events of 1982, and how he couldn't go with her ("it was easier for a congregation to accept the mother of an accused killer than the killer himself" p. 223.3–4), and he describes himself as having been "hungry for God" (p. 223.5). When he is in hospital after waking from the coma, and after Silas has been hospitalised following the showdown with Wallace, Angie invites Larry to attend her church, knowing that **religion is important to him** and that he has been shunned by the other congregations in the area (p. 307.11–14).

Loneliness has always permeated Larry's life and personality. When he was a young child, his mother used to pray together with him for God to bring him a special friend – **just one friend**. For a while this friend is Silas, a friendship largely conducted in secrecy, until Carl Ott forces the boys to fight, ruining their friendship for decades to come. Later, the role of "friend" is filled by Wallace Stringfellow – another strange outsider.

Alone and excluded

The loneliness which defines his life is seen in the novel in two phases: Prior to Cindy Walker's disappearance, he is an only child whose character and interests distance him from his peers, and whose rejection by his own father leaves him reliant on his mother and his internal life, e.g. his love of reading. After the events with Cindy Walker, Larry's loneliness is greatly amplified by his **ostracism**. The community around him completely rejects him, and he

3.4   Characters: Constellations & Characteristics

retreats into a life of almost total solitude in which, as he at one point notes, he can go for over a week with **no human contact** other than with the girls who work at Kentucky Fried Chicken (p. 261.27–29).

The defining event of Larry's life is the night in 1982 in which **Cindy Walker goes missing**. Larry has taken the girl out for the evening – thinking it's for a date at the drive-in – but she has manipulated him, and wants him to drive her to meet her secret boyfriend, by whom she claims to be pregnant. Larry does what she wants, but she vanishes and is never seen again. Larry is strongly suspected of having murdered her, but with no evidence and no body he is never charged or convicted. But everyone in the area knows of the case, and he becomes known as **"Scary Larry"** and is universally snubbed.

Night in 1982

When **Tina Rutherford** goes missing he is a prime suspect. While he is completely innocent, as he was of the disappearance and death of Cindy Walker, he once again is made to pay for the crime. Whereas the Walker case left him an outcast in his own home (largely due to Silas' unwillingness to tell the truth about that night in 1982), the Rutherford case sees him seriously wounded and comatose after being shot by the actual killer. The investigating detective Roy French suspects that Larry killed Tina Rutherford and then tried to shoot himself.

Suspected

Silas Jones

Silas is the son of Alice Jones and – as he only finds out much later in life – Carl Ott. He is widely known as "32" – he introduces himself as "32" at times (p. 186.32) because it was his number during his illustrious **school baseball career**. He is also known as Constable because of his job.

Athletic and smart

Silas is a police officer in Chabot. The position is neither particularly exciting nor is it well-paid. He has been doing the job for

3.4   Characters: Constellations & Characteristics

two years (p. 30.22) and has never had to fire his weapon or deal with a major crime. When he is first introduced it is clear that the department is under-equipped (p. 26.2–7) – for example, when he takes the Jeep he uses for work to be repaired, the mechanic in the garage says "If this thing was a horse we'd a done shot it" (p. 234.4–5).

Difficult relationship with his mother Alice

Silas **grew up in Chicago** with his mother and her boyfriend Oliver. When Oliver went on the run after getting in trouble with the police, Alice, who comes originally from Mississippi, moved back down south with Silas. Silas was 13 years old at the time. They lead a poverty-stricken, hard life for a long time, with Alice working multiple jobs. They **live for a while in the cabin on Ott's property** (see p. 57.16–24). Silas and his mother have a difficult relationship: He blames her for their problems and hates the way that she uses her looks and sexuality to manipulate men, although he understands, even as a child, that she does it in order to provide for him.

Friendship with Larry

Silas and Larry were good friends when they were children. Larry initiated the friendship, lending Silas a gun and teaching him how to shoot, as well as teaching him many other things **about life in rural Mississippi**. Their friendship is abruptly ended when Carl Ott discovers that Larry has given Silas the gun and forces them to fight over it. The stronger, bigger Silas easily beats Larry, who calls him "n****r" (p. 119), destroying their friendship for decades to come.

Silas and Cindy

Silas was Cindy Walker's **secret boyfriend**, and despite knowing that Larry was not responsible for her disappearance (Silas suspects it was Cecil, her stepfather, who killed her) he never comes forward to clear Larry's name, leaving his former friend to be treated as a pariah by everyone in the area for 25 years. It is only after Larry is shot and becomes a prime suspect in the disappearance of Tina Rutherford that Silas' girlfriend Angie forces the truth out of him.

3.4 Characters: Constellations & Characteristics

Cindy was infatuated with Silas, possibly because of the way that he ran to defend her from her abusive stepfather and the leering Carl Ott when they were taunting her (p. 110).

Silas' reaction to the Cindy's plight – he leaps up without hesitation to confront two drunk white men – demonstrate the bravery and **sense of righteousness** which form the core of his nature. Despite his terrible betrayal of Larry, leaving his former friend to be demonised by the entire community, he is a courageous and good man. His bravery costs him dearly later when he confronts Wallace Stringfellow alone and is savagely attacked by the dog John Wayne Gacy.

Brave

Silas ruined his arm playing baseball. He entered the navy and got to see many different parts of the world. He had never planned on becoming a police officer: He responded to a job vacancy advertisement for a "constable in a hamlet" because he liked the words (see p. 54 for Silas reflecting on his life after high school). He is **tall, strong, athletic, good-looking and charismatic**. He makes friends easily and people like him. Women find him attractive.

Half-brother of Larry

While investigating the disappearance of Tina Rutherford and the attempted murder of Larry Ott, Silas eventually focuses his suspicions on Wallace Stringfellow. During the **showdown at Wallace's home**, Silas is badly wounded when Wallace sets his monstrous dog on him. During his investigations he learns that Carl Ott was his father and that Larry is therefore his half-brother.

Carl Ott

Carl is **cruel and callous**, and appears to be a **genuine sadist**, taking delight in other people being hurt. This can be seen in his anecdote about Cecil falling in the thorn bushes (pp. 155–158) as well as in Silas' recollection of Larry having told him how much Carl enjoyed it when Larry got hit by a stone thrown out by the lawnmower (p. 188).

Larry's father, husband of Ina, and the true father of Silas Jones

He also appears to be aroused by **Cecil** Walker's attempts to sexually humiliate his stepdaughter Cindy (pp. 109–110). He tells stories in which his principal enjoyment seems to come from the misfortunes or sufferings of others (pp. 64–67).

Fight between both sons

The strongest example of his **cruel nature** can be seen when he forces Larry and Silas to fight one another for possession of the gun (pp.116–120). He whips Larry with a belt when he refuses to fight back. His sadism is on full display when he tells the boys they can "bite if they want to […] fight dirty" (p. 119.16–19).

Carl was involved with **Alice Jones**, mother of Silas, and Larry finds out much, much later that **Carl is Silas' real father**. When Alice and Silas return to Chabot, Carl lets them live in the cabin on his property. Until Larry lets his mother know what is going on, Carl also picks up Alice and Silas when he drives Larry to school in the mornings.

Storyteller

Carl is tall and athletic. He has blond curly hair, dark skin and green eyes (p. 62.30–31). Aside from his cruelty and domineering nature, the most prominent aspect of his personality is his love of telling stories to an attentive audience. Larry has clear memories of being in his father's repair shop and listening to him **talking for hours to his circle of friends**, telling the same stories over and over again because the others enjoy them so much (pp. 64–67). Carl Ott eventually dies in a drunk driving accident.

Ina Jean Ott

Larry's mother

She is a gentler creature than her husband Carl, and tried to help Larry deal with his loneliness. She is **devoted to her son** and prayed for him to find a friend when he was a child (pp. 113–115). Later, when Larry returns from military service and after Carl dies in a drunk driving accident, Larry moves her into a nursing home. She has developed dementia and can no longer focus on times and people. Silas tries occasionally to talk to her to learn more about the truth of his parentage.

Ina becomes suspicious of **Carl's contacts with Alice Jones** and tries to find out more by questioning Larry (pp. 58–61). She knows that the two had an affair – see her comments to Alice (p. 61.13–14) and to Carl (p. 113.5–13). But when Silas talks to her in the nursing home she doesn't appear to know who fathered Alice's baby (pp. 238–239).

Betrayed wife

Alice Jones

Alice Jones originally came from Mississippi, and she moved to Chicago when she became pregnant with Silas (the father is Carl Ott). She had been **working as a maid for the Otts** and taking care of Larry as a baby (p. 130). Larry's mother Ina remembers her when Silas shows her a photo: "A nice colored girl, but loose. She got herself in a family way and wasn't married." (p. 238.22–23)

Silas' mother

Alice works hard to support Silas and herself – when Silas and Larry meet in the woods for the first time, Silas tells Larry that his mother works two jobs (at the Piggly Wiggly supermarket, and as a waitress at a diner in Fulsom p. 78.12–14).

Silas is bothered by his mother's relationships with men – how she uses her good looks to make men do what she wants ("men noticed Alice Jones" p. 131.28). She does this **to provide for her and for Silas**. He also believes that he is an obstacle to her: "Silas knew what the bus driver wanted with his mother, and he thought how he, Silas, was in a way an impediment. Without him here, she could do whatever she needed to, without witness, to get through this cold night, to get wherever she was going. He knew his mother was beautiful." (p. 137.20–24) It is worth remembering that Silas is only 13 when he thinks this: At such a young age he already understands his mother's transactional approach to life – **she of-**

Good looking

3.4 Characters: Constellations & Characteristics

fers herself, her beauty and her body, in return for transportation, shelter, protection – and we can see him already taking on some of her cold, hard perspective.

Protects Silas

Silas understands that his mother is "starving from loneliness" (p. 192.24–25), but he refuses to show sympathy for her or help her in any way. And while Silas does know that she does all she can to provide for him and to protect him, he resents it deeply. He has a tendency – as a boy and later as a man – to maintain an **emotional distance** from other people. He is charming and friendly but some of his **mother's hardness** remains inside him.

Alice and Carl

It is this tendency and ability of hers which led to Silas – he is the result of her affair with Carl Ott. Carl, a dominant and powerful physical presence, was obviously drawn to the beautiful young Alice, and she responded. Since she later returns to him for help – he provides her with the cabin and buys her a car – it can be assumed that their relationship was consensual and that Carl did not rape her or take advantage of her.

Courageously

Alice is a tough woman. Silas experiences her hardness when he is young – she slaps him for asking too many questions (pp. 135–136) and impresses on him how hard the world is ("Don't you dare run [...] from the one person in this world who love you," p. 136.6–7). When she and Silas leave Chicago **she has nothing**: She is forced to sell her last possessions to buy bus tickets to get them further south after her initial plan to settle in Memphis (Tennessee) fell through. **She obviously does not want to return to Chabot.**

Died eight years before the present-day events of the novel

Alice's toughness comes from her **isolation** and her constant, lifelong struggle to maintain both herself and her son: "You ain't seen it that bad. I know. I know cause I have seen it that bad. But you. Up till now you had it easier than I ever did." (pp. 141.32–142.2) She lacks the gentle warmth of Larry's mother Ina, and consequently the support and lessons she provides for Silas are very different from

3.4 Characters: Constellations & Characteristics

Ina's support for Larry. In the same conversation (pp. 141–143) she says that maybe she was wrong to not have treated Silas worse – that she maybe was too soft on him, and that his current ingratitude is a result of her not having forced him to see the difficulties of life to a greater extent. These are under any circumstances tough words for a 13-year old to hear from their mother.

Alice disapproves of **Silas' relationship with Cindy Walker** (p. 246.19) and she sends him away to a different school when she learns that, despite her warning and his promise, he has continued to see her (p. 248.6–13).

Wallace Stringfellow

"You know me, Larry. I'm a outlaw. Can't do it legal or it's no fun."
(Wallace, p. 282.30–31)

Wallace is mentioned in the first chapter when Larry thinks about "Wallace Stringfellow [...] who was his only friend." (p. 22.21–22) He reappears later in the novel, first when Silas pulls him over because of his **erratic driving** (p. 190). He has by this time already turned up at Larry's farm pretending to be a TV engineer (p. 198), after which the **two outcasts become friends**.

Larry first noticed signs of Wallace having **trespassed on his property** when he was 31, ten years before Tina Rutherford went missing (p. 195.1–3). Although he only realises much later, when Wallace returns as an adult, the boy he scares off with his zombie mask is Wallace, already as a boy fascinated by the horrors of Scary Larry.

Fascinated by "Scary Larry"

Wallace is in his early 20s, a little under six feet tall, with a scruffy beard and unshaven face. He is thin and bony and dresses in dirty and worn clothing. He drinks a lot and smokes a lot of marijuana: He

"White trash": Sex and drugs

3.4   Characters: Constellations & Characteristics

also appears to be involved with other drugs. He is dirty and **unhygienic, uneducated and poor**. He lives in a squalid little house near a catfish farm. He used to live with his mother, who gives him advice and tells him what to do: "Momma keeps saying get my GED…" (p. 201.15–16), "Momma said get rid of em…" (p. 207.24). She has different boyfriends ("One of Momma's boyfriends…"p. 208.1) and is a regular churchgoer (p. 211.23–30). She is also promiscuous, and Wallace has obviously listened closely to her having sex with her boyfriends (see 219.15–17).

Dog John Wayne Gacy

He has a dog, an **aggressive pit bull-Chow** cross-breed called John Wayne Gacy. The dog is constantly described as "mean" and Wallace uses it like a weapon to try and kill Silas (see pp. 294–295).

> **John Wayne Gacy** (1942–1994) was an American serial killer who was convicted of having raped, tortured and killed 33 teenaged boys in Cook County, Illinois (a suburb of Chicago) in the 1970s. He was known as the "Killer Clown" because he frequently worked as a clown, including at children's parties. The significance of the dog's name is both intentional and coincidental: primarily, it illustrates Wallace's fascination with rape and murder, a very important key to his identity as the killer of Tina Rutherford. There is also an unnerving coincidental link to Silas, who grew up in Chicago, the site of Gacy's crimes.
>
> And as if being named after a serial killer wasn't bad enough, the dog is also referred to as "Cujo" (p. 290.27) by Silas, a reference to the eponymous murderously rabid canine villain of the Stephen King novel.

3.4 Characters: Constellations & Characteristics

When he was a child Wallace sneaked onto Larry's property on numerous occasions, fiddling with things in the barn and stealing things (pp. 195–197). Larry ambushes him, wearing **the zombie mask**, in an effort to scare him away for good. Years later, when Wallace comes back to his property, Larry recognises the boy from back then in the young man. They become friends. Both are very **damaged and lonely individuals**, but what becomes clear is that Wallace is drawn to Larry by his obsession with rape and murder. He was drawn as a child to the idea of "Scary Larry", who was believed to have raped and murdered Cindy Walker.

After Wallace has shot Larry and Larry is lying in a coma in hospital, Wallace **begins to hang around the hospital**, lurking and trying to find out more about Larry's status (pp. 232.15–233.3, 234.9–22).

Wallace is the **killer of Tina Rutherford**, probably the murderer of M&M, and he is also the masked home **invader who shoots Larry**. He stages the shooting of Larry to make it look like a suicide (he leaves the gun in Larry's hand). He is eventually tracked down by Silas. He sets John Wayne Gacy on Silas and runs away to be later caught in a shootout with sheriff's deputies, during which he kills himself.

Larry and Wallace

Criminal

Cindy Walker

Cecil Walker's step-daughter and daughter of Shelia Walker. In 1982, Cindy Walker went missing, presumed dead, and **her body was never discovered**. It was widely believed that Larry Ott was responsible for her death as he was the only person known to have been with her the night she vanished. Twenty-five years later, the truth comes out: She also saw Silas Jones that night, and was almost certainly killed by her step-father, Cecil. She has premonitions of the danger she's in – "That Cecil's after me," (p. 162.7), "if Cecil

Silas' secret girlfriend

3.4 Characters: Constellations & Characteristics

finds out [that she's pregnant] he'll kill me" (p. 162.28–29) – and she hates and fears him.

She is thin and has curly blonde hair and blue eyes and freckles (p. 242.22–30). Cindy is a few years older than Larry. He is fascinated by her beauty and **loves to spy on her** when she is sunbathing (p. 68.11–26).

Sexual object and "white trash"

Cindy is objectified by the men and boys around her. Her step-father's attitude towards her is domineering, predatory and un-healthy in its sexually motivated hostility. Even Larry says of her: "She'd been his secret, but maybe it was time to share her." (p. 104.12), which implies that she is an **object to be admired**, a kind of possession, rather than a real person. She is obviously deeply infatuated with Silas, but he doesn't share the depth of her feelings – he seems to be having a good time with her, exploit-ing her open sexuality and her need to be loved and wanted. She spends a lot of time watching him play baseball and he enjoys the attention from this sexually aware white girl (pp. 241–247 – see also p. 244.27–28, "He was a virgin but she wasn't").

She claims to be pregnant in order to pressure Larry into helping her, knowing that he will respond to such an extreme situation, but she was probably not pregnant (p. 247.21–28).

Other characters
Angie Baker

Silas' girlfriend, an EMT[9]

Angie is also black. She loves Silas very much and makes efforts to understand why he is lying to her. She is unpretentious, direct and honest. One thing Silas likes about her is that "she never wore makeup or did her nails" (175.4–5).

---

9   EMT: emergency medical technician – specially trained medical personnel who ride in ambu-lances to provide emergency medical care.

Angie is also **very clever**: She sees the holes in Silas' stories about his relationships with Larry and with Cindy Walker immediately (pp. 178–181). She knows that Silas is lying to her. She listens to what Silas tells her of Larry having been such a loser and outsider at school, and immediately asks about Larry and Cindy's date – "Why'd she go? If he was such a loser?" (p. 181.9). She also forces him to tell her about his past with Cindy Walker, and she challenges him to make things right with Larry, making him see that for the last 25 years Larry has suffered because of Silas's inability to tell the truth (pp. 240–249).

Roy French

The tough and experienced Gerald County chief investigator French is the detective who is **investigating the disappearance of Tina Rutherford**. French has a large and loud personality. He is a meticulous worker and tries to teach Silas how to conduct basic investigative and forensic tasks, like taking prints of tire tracks, for example. He used to work as a game warden and is a veteran of the Vietnam War (1955–1975). He is known for his talents as an investigator, and in particular for his ability to coerce confessions (see p. 263.1–7).

Chief investigator

French is in his late fifties. He is tall and thin with green eyes and red hair and moustache. He often wears t-shirts with pro-gun rights slogans ("YOU HAVE THE RIGHT TO REMAIN SILENT FOREVER" p. 33.20–21, "GUN CONTROL MEANS HITTING WHERE YOU AIM" p. 297.30–31).

French is convinced from the earliest stages of the investigation into Larry's shooting that he shot himself (p. 91.7) out of guilt for having murdered Tina Rutherford (as well as Cindy Walker and possibly other girls through the years – pp. 257–262).

3.4   Characters: Constellations & Characteristics

Morton Morrisette

"M&M": drug
dealer

Usually referred to as "M&M". He is a local **marijuana dealer** who is at first believed to have been murdered by Charles Deacon. It later turns out that he was almost certainly murdered by Wallace Stringfellow (p. 309.4–7).

Silas and M&M were good friends at school and they played baseball together: "The double-play combo was locally famous, 32 Jones and M&M, two youngsters, the newspaper had said, you couldn't get a ball between if you shot it out of a gun." (p. 149.26–29)

Morrisette used to work for the Rutherford Lumber Mill but hurt his back and lived on a disability allowance from then on, earning extra money by dealing in marijuana. He is believed to have been active as a drug dealer since the early 1990s. He drove a Chevy Impala, which was discovered a few days before Silas found his corpse in the swamp (Chapter 2, pp. 26–36), a burning wreck. Roy French and the local narcotics investigator suspected a local crack addict, Charles Deacon, of having murdered Morrisette.

Tina Rutherford

Local girl, 19 years old, a student at the University of Mississippi in Oxford, Mississippi (colloquially known as "Ole Miss"), and the daughter of a wealthy family who own the largest company and major employer in the area, the Rutherford Lumber Mill. When the novel begins, Tina is missing, feared dead.

Kidnapped and
murdered

Larry is suspected of having something to do with her disappearance, but as it turns out, Wallace Stringfellow kidnapped, raped and murdered her. Silas discovers her body buried under a bed in the old cabin on the Ott property where he and his mother used to live.

"The Rutherford girl had been missing for eight days" are the first words in the novel, making it clear what the focus of the novel,

3.4 Characters: Constellations & Characteristics

specifically as a work of crime fiction, is going to be. She is mentioned again in the first chapter when Larry is watching the morning news on TV (p. 21.13).

Cecil Walker

Cecil is an **admirer of Carl Ott** and hangs around him a lot (see pp. 64–67). Cecil is an abusive drunkard who refuses to work after claiming to have hurt his back working at the Rutherford mill (p. 108.22–24). He is a foolish man who can be tricked into doing dangerous and humiliating things – see pp. 155–158 for Carl's anecdote about a humiliating and potentially extremely dangerous stunt he paid Cecil to perform.

Stepfather to Cindy Walker

He has an unhealthy **sexual desire for his stepdaughter**, which most commonly manifests in violence and rage. He openly calls her "you little whore" (p. 160.3) in front of Larry. Cindy describes to Silas how he tries to see her naked and constantly harasses her (pp. 245.14–246.5).

On the night in 1982 when Larry is supposed to take Cindy to the drive-in, Cecil threatens and manhandles Larry (pp. 158.17–160.18), physically assaulting the boy and threatening to castrate him if he touches Cindy.

Although the truth is never fully revealed in the novel, it appears most likely that it was Cecil who killed and disposed of Cindy Walker back in 1982. Cecil died of cancer some years before the present day events of the novel (p. 269.14).

Cecil is suspected of killing Cindy

Miss Voncille

The **town clerk** Voncille is a white woman in her early 50s who has been divorced twice already (p. 37). She shares office space with Silas and is the most senior official in the town of Chabot. She is

Saves Silas' life

3.4 Characters: Constellations & Characteristics

responsible for saving Silas' life after his showdown with Wallace Stringfellow, sending sheriff's deputies to back him up.

Morris Sheffield
Mayor, real estate agent and volunteer firefighter. He comes to the mayor's office in Chabot Town Hall a couple of times a day, but Silas rarely sees him except for at "monthly office meetings and the occasional fire" (p. 37.15–16).

Olivia
Postal worker (pp. 49–53) with whom Silas had a brief affair.

Irina Mott
Young woman (22 or 23 years old) who lives on "White Trash Avenue" (Fourteenth Avenue) in Fulsom. She calls Silas out to deal with a snake which has been put in her mailbox (pp. 49–53). While he is despatching the snake they flirt with one another. Later in the novel, she and Silas get drunk together and nearly sleep together (pp. 273–277). She tells him about her friend Evelyn, who had been briefly involved with Wallace Stringfellow, whom she believes put the snake in her mailbox. The details she provides put Silas on the trail to Wallace as the prime suspect in the shooting of Larry and Tina Rutherford's disappearance.

Evelyn
Although we never see Evelyn in the novel, she has an **important role** to play. She is first mentioned by Wallace on one of his visits to Larry: "I'm single, too. But it's a ole gal over in Fulsom? I see her once in a while. Evelyn. One a them on-again, off-again situations." (p. 209.21–23) Irina Mott tells Silas about Evelyn's involvement with

3.4 Characters: Constellations & Characteristics

a creepy skinny white guy who keeps snakes (pp. 274.17–275.27). This inspires Silas to investigate Wallace Stringfellow.

Shelia Walker
Cindy's mother and Cecil's wife – a "mouse of a mother" (p. 244.6). She works the night shift at the tie factory in Fulsom (p. 109.13–14). She probably saves Larry's life on the night of Cindy's disappearance when she returns home from work just as Cecil is strangling the boy (p. 168.20–25).

Uncle Colin
Ina Ott's brother, Larry's uncle. Uncle Colin is described early in the novel (p. 62), and while he has no role in the plot, he serves to further illustrate Carl Ott's character. As a vegetarian and a more urbane, sophisticated man than the crude Carl, Colin is immediately suspect and seems to Carl to be somehow less of a man than he should be. Carl's disgusted, hostile reaction to anything outside his own nature is indicative of his intolerance and brutish personality.

Charles Deacon
Local crackhead (addicted to crack cocaine) alleged to have murdered Morrisette.

Tab Johnson
Angie's driver. He suspects, like Roy French, that Larry shot himself in a suicide attempt (p. 176.4–5).

Shannon Knight
Police reporter, the only journalist Silas talks to when the Rutherford case is solved following the showdown with Wallace Stringfellow (p. 310.6–14).

3.4 Characters: Constellations & Characteristics

Jackie Simmons

Black girl at school. Larry is tricked into being rude to her (calling her "Monkey Lips") in a misguided attempt to ingratiate himself with two white boys, Ken and David.

Carolyn

A black girl in Larry's class at school who beats him up after he racially insults her friend Jackie Simmons (pp. 74.16–75.25).

Marla

Waitress in The Hub (pp. 121–123). Marla is the only character we see who shows compassion for Larry ("I always felt bad for him", p. 123.3) and who refuses to be swept along with the general distrust and condemnation. She evens fires a girl who worked for her because she told Larry he wasn't welcome in The Hub.

Oliver

Alice Jones' boyfriend in Chicago (pp. 131–133). He was in trouble with the police and fled, leaving Alice, who then decided to move back down south with Silas. Silas has mixed memories of Oliver, not all positive. They lived together for nearly seven years – a substantial portion of Silas's childhood.

Jon Davidson

"Jon with no 'h'" does volunteer work at the hospital. He is a humorous older white man with whom Silas has an easy and friendly relationship. Jon Davidson is a nice example of a character in a novel with a singular and clear function: To provide Silas with information to move the plot along. He appears four times in the novel – he is briefly introduced (p. 181) and the friendly relationship between him and Silas is established. He tells Silas that Wallace has been to

3.4   Characters: Constellations & Characteristics

the hospital to check on Larry (pp. 232.1–233.3). He is also the one
to call Silas to tell him when Larry wakes from the coma (p. 251).
He also calls Silas to inform him that Larry has left the hospital
(p. 318.8–27).

Sheriff Jack Lolly

Investigating the Rutherford disappearance together with Roy
French. Lolly is mentioned by French early on, when he and Silas
are investigating Larry's house (p. 90.18–20), and he appears in the
novel towards the end, when he and French interview Larry. They
try to persuade Larry to confess to having murdered Tina Rutherford and then attempted suicide. Lolly had taken Larry's guns away
from him after his father's death – it is implied that this was done
with no legal authority ("Took em away how?" – "Just did it.").

Devoid Chapman

A black man who features in various anecdotes told by Carl Ott
(pp. 64–67).

Ken and David

Two white boys at school who manipulate Larry into being rude to
a black girl, Jackie Simmons (pp. 69–75). They figure in minor roles
in Larry's history, typically as unwelcome troublemakers.

Constellations

Larry is the focus of the novel – the central character and the person
around whom the plot revolves, in the past as well as in the present.
Larry is an extremely **isolated figure**, yet everyone in the novel is to
some degree or another connected to him. His status as main suspect
in the disappearances of both Cindy Walker and Tina Rutherford
means that everyone has an opinion about him or is actively involved

3.4 Characters: Constellations & Characteristics

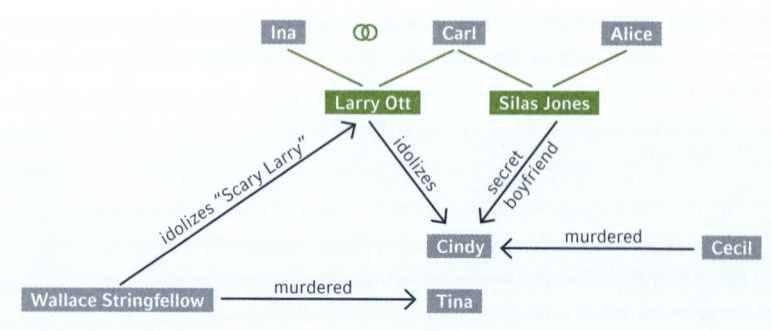

in investigating him. He is the focus of the novel in the events of both 1982 and the present day, even though he is in both cases an accidental agent and not a protagonist.

Chronology

Another very important factor is that the **chronology** of the novel focuses on two different periods in time: 1982 and the present day. The constellations of the characters shift through time. Here there are reflections of the situation – the same central figures and a young girl gone missing – with the same suspect (Larry). There are however also "negative" reflections, with Silas in the older case being the one who condemns Larry through his silence while saving him in the present, and Cecil (the probable murderer) in the older case not being identified or caught, while Wallace (the killer in the present day) is identified and killed.

Family affairs

A further way to organise the characters which reflects the symmetry of the novel's structure, plot(s) and characters is with **Carl Ott** at the centre. Carl is the father of both Larry and Silas and, as a quite literal point of origin for the entire story, he can be used as a focal point around which to arrange the two sides of most of

3.4 Characters: Constellations & Characteristics

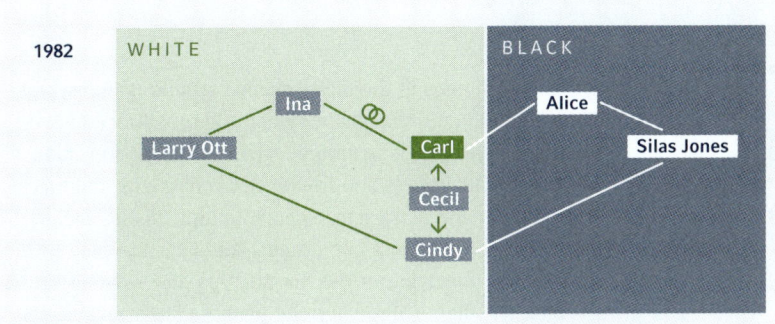

the major aspects of the book: black/white, then/now, Cindy/Tina, Walker/Rutherfords.

The novel contains **a triangle of brothers**, both real and symbolic: Larry, Silas and Wallace. Larry and Silas are half-brothers and Wallace is a kind of shadowy, twisted symbolic brother to Larry. Wallace shoots Larry and Wallace and Silas almost kill one another as Silas – in addition to doing his job – is in a way trying to avenge Larry.

Larry, Silas and Wallace

3.5 Themes

SUMMARY

The major themes in the novel revolve around memory and the past, guilt and responsibility and the broad idea of "belonging". Belonging is an umbrella theme, which covers many other areas: loneliness and friendship, community and race, social status and ostracism. Specific minor themes include power, horror, kindness and cruelty. And as is the case with most fiction involving crime, friendships and secrets from the past, the theme of redemption plays an important role in *Crooked Letter*.

These themes are entwined in complex ways: many of the examples from the text discussed below are relevant to more than one of the thematic areas identified.

The themes at a glance:
→ Memory, the past and secrets
→ Guilt, responsibility and betrayal
→ Power
→ Belonging
→ Horror and monsters
→ Redemption

Memory, the past and secrets

Childhood and adulthood

The story of *Crooked Letter, Crooked Letter* unfolds in **two different time periods**. In the past (1979–1982), we have secrets (Silas' parentage, what happened the night Cindy disappeared), a crime (the disappearance of Cindy Walker) and a betrayal (Larry and Silas –

3.5 Themes

the fight, the insult, and Silas' silence), and in the present day we have a second, similar crime – the disappearance and murder of Tina Rutherford – and the overcoming of the old betrayal through the revelation of the secrets.

The two time frames are very significant for the development of the characters. Both Silas and Larry (and other characters around them) have been **frozen in time** by what happened in 1982, unable to escape the crimes and betrayals. For as long as there are secrets and unacknowledged guilt, there can be no confession, forgiveness or resolution of the events of that time.

No resolution

Prisoners of the past, frozen in time:

TEXT	PP.	ANALYSIS
"I believe our victim here's the last resident in Mississippi without a remote control. [...] Unusual fellow. A frozen in the 1960s kind of character. [...] My guess is he ain't touched this particular room since his momma went to the home."	90–95	Silas and Roy French investigate Larry's house. The past is of central importance in the novel. Larry has been frozen in time by the events of 1982. He lives where he was born and has been unable to leave. He goes through the motions of continuing his father's work at the repair shop (without having updated his tools or methods, as French notes – see 91.25–31) and maintains his mother's routines for caring for her chickens.
Shelves full of the books Larry had read as a kid. [...] ... rows of suits and shirts, clothes of a boy on one end and growing longer down the rod, a man on the other.	86.22–87.1	Larry surrounds himself with the books he read as a child and his wardrobe still contains the clothes he has worn through his life from boyhood to manhood (86.29–87.2).

3.5 Themes

TEXT	PP.	ANALYSIS
Their lives had stopped, frozen ...	171.12	In the time after Cindy's disappearance and with all suspicion falling on Larry, the Ott family is frozen in time. The family will never recover from this, with Carl becoming an alcoholic and dying in a car crash and Larry's mother withdrawing into herself until Alzheimer's takes her.
...going too fast for him to notice consequences...	272.24–273.6	Silas also thinks about this idea of being frozen in time. After confessing to Larry about the night Cindy disappeared, he sits alone in the diner and remembers being a child, travelling to school. "Everything froze," he says, wondering if childhood was a blur of constant motion, and adulthood a state of being frozen: he sees himself as a man in his 40s, frozen in time and being hit by the rush of past events.
"You can bury the past but it always seems to come back, one way or another." "The only way you'll ever feel better about this is to own up and pay the price." "We was just telling Larry here that his guilt won't go away until he owns up to what he's done."	260.22–23 262.7–6 265.4–6	Both men, Larry and Silas, have been immobilised in different ways by the events of 1982. While Larry has most obviously and fundamentally been frozen, Silas has also struggled to deal with a sense of guilt and responsibility. As Roy French points out in the quotations provided here, you can only move forward once you have confessed. He is addressing Larry, but the insight is more relevant to Silas. He is guilty of having ruined Larry's life – or contributed to the destruction of Larry's life – and has to confess in order to leave this guilt behind him.

3.5 Themes

TEXT	PP.	ANALYSIS
Silas inhaled, a man now, full of unknowns yet, but, maybe, with some future still ahead.	314.23–24	It is only after he has confessed to Larry and has begun atoning for the damage his silence has caused, and after returning the rifle to Larry's house, that Silas begins to feel like he has "some future still ahead". The guilt he has been feeling has prevented him from moving on with his life – in a less obvious way than has been the case with Larry, but no less profound. To different degrees, both Larry and Silas have been unable to become "men" by what happened in 1982. They have remained boys. Larry, literally surrounded by his childhood, physically rooted in childhood, and Silas, emotionally immature and unable to acknowledge and confront his guilt. This passage on p. 314 illustrates how Silas has finally become able to feel like he is now (at the age of 40-something) a man.
How long he'd waited on his porch [...], rereading the same books [...], waiting for Silas and Cindy to return ...	279.26–280.24	Having woken from his coma, Larry becomes increasingly aware of how he has been a prisoner of the past. The revelation of Silas' betrayal and the fact that it had cost Larry a full 25 years of his life only makes this feeling worse: he has fallen out of the world, which has progressed without him, leaving him stuck in limbo. He thinks about "this world [he] hadn't caught up to" (284.7) and in the par-

3.5 Themes

TEXT	PP.	ANALYSIS
		ticularly poignant passage referenced here, looks back on his life, which he now sees has been wasted. He has been unable and unwilling to enter the world and participate in its changing.

The passage of time

Larry: prisoner of the past

Larry is a prisoner of the past, while time and the world have continued to move around him. The final crisis of the novel's plot – the showdown between Silas and Wallace, with all that follows, including Larry's complete exoneration from all suspicion of the crimes – frees him from the past. He will now be able to join the world and once again to move with the passage of time.

There are numerous passages in *Crooked Letter* which touch on the idea of what the world had once been – further reinforcing the significance of past events for the characters and plot of the novel. This idea is very closely tied to the fundamental idea of the loss of innocence. Both Larry and Silas had had moments of happiness as children, and the events of 1982 had robbed both of them, in different ways, of all innocence and happiness.

3.5 Themes

TEXT	PP.	ANALYSIS
But watching its images, he was catching up to what the world had become. No more the world of green leaves where his father had carried a shotgun to school [...]. Summers Carl Ott had gone shirtless and grown dark brown from the sun … Now the land had been clear-cut. [...] The sun burned its cancer into your skin, and if you brought a gun to school it was to murder your classmates.	284.9–18	Larry has been stuck in the world of his childhood, but the world around him has changed. It is in many ways, as this passage illustrates, a darker, more dangerous world now. An uncomplicated relationship with the natural world is no longer possible, and gun violence has reached epidemic levels.
… Larry lay amid his machines, thinking of Silas, how time packs new years over the old ones but how those old years are still in there, like the earliest, tightest rings centering a tree, the most hidden, enclosed in darkness and shielded from weather.	300.7–11	Larry's reflections on the passing of time show that he understands not only how time has passed him by but how he has been frozen in time, held in the "darkness" of the "earliest, tightest" ring of years.
For a moment he held the old rifle [...]. It seemed lighter than it used to be. [...] Holding it for a moment he was a boy again, the world the world it had been a long time ago, a world full of unknowns, a world full of future and possibility …	314.11–27	Like Larry, Silas feels a nostalgia for the less complicated, less dangerous world of his childhood: but this passage makes it clearer that it is not the world and the environment of the past that he yearns for, but the unexplored potential of who he had been as a child. Looking back on his life after having made so many mistakes and having seen the damage he has

3.5   Themes

TEXT	PP.	ANALYSIS
		caused, Silas longs to have less knowledge of the struggle and pain of being human.
They passed through the quiet Fulsom town square, the hardware store now a tanning salon [...]. The drugstore a video rental place [...]. Two closed barbershops ...	319.30–320.2	Silas and Larry are driving through town and seeing the changes since they were children. This is an interesting passage: they are not two men returning to their childhood hometown having been away for 25 years: they are two men who live here and will have seen these changes occurring over the years. But they still perceive a transition from the landscape of their childhood memories to the reality of their adult lives. This passage is symbolically significant in its illustration of how the two central characters perceive and interact with the passage of time in the real world.

Memories and flashbacks

Two timelines A lot of the novel is told in flashbacks, and Larry and Silas often both think back on past events, letting them illuminate and explain the events of the present. See the relevant section in Chapter 3.3 Structure in this book for more on the chronology of the story and the way the two timelines are structured, as well as taking a closer look at the significance of the two timelines and the relevance of the flashbacks as a literary device.

Memories are also inextricably linked to the secrets hidden in the past. Here are some specific examples from the text of how memories are used to address themes and ideas.

3.5   Themes

TEXT	PP.	ANALYSIS
He pulled the chain that raised the bay door and stood watching the highway, struck by a memory. [...] ... he'd gone right past here and from the car window seen Larry standing where Silas stood now, in this spot. Silas had kept his eyes forward, as if Larry could've seen him, as if he'd been standing there all those years, watching for Silas to come back. It had bothered him ...	124.27–125.12	This scene reinforces the symmetry so often seen in the book. Silas is standing where Larry stands, in Ottomotive Repairs, watching the street as Larry always did. In addition, here is further evidence of Silas' awareness and repression of his guilty conscience.
Twenty-five years later, his head full of the past [...]. Silas stared at the photograph of his mother. ... this was the first picture he'd seen of her in decades [...]. ... this plastic smile, the photograph, was better than no picture at all.	143.26–144.7	When they leave Chicago for the South, Silas and his mother lose all of their possessions, including all of their family photographs. Silas has a very complex relationship with his mother, and it is another part of his life (in addition to Larry and Cindy) about which he feels very guilty. The events of the novel from the shooting of Larry onwards force Silas to re-examine his own past, to confront memories he has avoided, and finally to come to peace with his own past actions.
[Wallace on how fascinated he had been by Larry when he was a boy]	210.17–213.14	Larry knows that Wallace was the boy who had trespassed on his property a few years ago. Wallace admits it, and goes on to talk about how he had been fascinated by Larry – "Scary Larry" – as a boy. Wallace remembers things extremely clearly, illustrating the personal obsession behind the re-

3.5 Themes

TEXT	PP.	ANALYSIS
		lationship, and his memories also provide more insight into how ostracised and outcast Larry has become since the events of 1982 – up to the point of his not even being welcome in church anymore.
He'd avoided it so long himself it sometimes didn't even seem real, what had happened in 1982.	230.16–17	Silas has distanced himself from his own memories to such a degree that they no longer seem real. The "it" he is talking about here is the truth about Cindy and the night she disappeared. He can barely acknowledge it even in the privacy of his own mind.
"I came to ask you about my mother," he said. [...] "...that was our maid [...]. Alice Jones. But she had to leave [...]. I remember you, Silas. You were Larry's friend. [...] Silas ? [...] I'm frightened."	238.11– 239.11	Silas visits Ina Ott in the nursing home. Ina suffers from Alzheimer's (a degenerative brain disease which affects memory, among many other things) and her memory is extremely unreliable, but on this visit she recalls Alice and remembers that Silas and Larry had been friends as boys. Her mind is troubled by things she can no longer identify or understand – when she says that Alice had been "loose" she is forgetting that her husband Carl had also been "loose". Both Ina and Silas are troubled by their memories of the past, but only Silas can still uncover the truth and atone for it.
The benefit – she would have said blessing – of her Alzheimer's was that the first swath of history gone from her memory was the incident with Cindy Walker and its longreaching aftermath.	195.19–21	For all of the characters in the story, the past is a dark place full of pain and regret. For Ina Ott it is now out of reach: she has forgotten her husband's infidelity, the suspicions about her son, which destroyed his life and their family, and the disappearance of Cindy Walker.

3.5 Themes

TEXT	PP.	ANALYSIS
		The loss of her memories is a kind of "blessing" but it is also very final: it means that she can never make peace with the past. Silas and Larry on the other hand must face the past and explore their memories in order to be able to move on with their lives. Ina Ott's life, robbed of memories and knowledge of the past, is essentially over.

Secrets

People around Larry have a lot of secrets. His father, Silas, Cindy and Wallace – all keep secrets from him to a greater or lesser extent, and these secrets have **wide-ranging implications** for Larry and his life.

Impact on Larry

TEXT	PP.	ANALYSIS
She'd been his secret, but maybe it was time to share her.	104.12	Larry spies on Cindy and considers her to be in a way "his". This objectification and possessiveness is a little unnerving: while he has neither Wallace's murderous fantasies nor Cecil's sexual aggression, Larry is seen here thinking of Cindy as an object, whose only purpose is to be there for his pleasure. He keeps this voyeuristic relationship a secret until he decides to "share her" with Silas. Sharing this "secret" however leads to Silas and Cindy coming together and her eventual disappearance.

3.5 Themes

TEXT	PP.	ANALYSIS
The bottom drawer held only a shoe box full of old photographs. [...] One photo at the bottom showed baby Larry in a woman's lap. [...] ... the thing that stunned Silas, the thing he couldn't believe, was that this woman was his mother.	129.28–130.29	Here, Silas is going back into Larry's past and his memories, and in the end he discovers the secret of his father's identity. This passage is relevant to all of the memory and guilt-related themes in the novel, but it is most significant as the moment when one of the most important secrets in the story is revealed.
"Listen," she said. "You have to help me. [...] ... swear to God you won't never tell nobody. [...] I'm gonna have a baby [...]. You the only person in the world who can help me, Larry."	162.6–163.26	Cindy makes Larry promise to never tell what she is planning to do that night in 1982. There are two secrets here: the real one and the fake one. The fake one is her pregnancy: she is not expecting Silas' baby. The real one is the meeting with Silas, which she has to engineer using Larry to conceal the truth from Cecil. The fact that Larry obeys her instructions and (at least at first) doesn't admit to the police what he knows weighs very heavily against him and makes him look much more guilty than he actually is.
[Silas remembering Cindy]	241–247	There is a lot of significant material in this lengthy memory, and it is relevant here for the secrecy of their relationship. The two are treated with suspicion and concern by white people: Silas' mother is deeply opposed to it: Cindy has to conceal it from Cecil: Silas even keeps it secret from his best friend, M&M. Cindy keeps it secret from Larry, using him as a tool to allow her to meet secretly with Silas. The secrecy of the liaison

3.5 Themes

TEXT	PP.	ANALYSIS
		means that, without Silas telling the truth, Larry will spend the rest of his life ostracised and demonised as a suspected murderer and that the Ott family will be destroyed.
"Is there something you want to say, then?" French asked. Here it all came. A quarter of a century bunching up on him, bearing down, a truck slamming on its brakes and its logs sliding forward, over the cab, through the window, the back of his head, shooting past him on the road. "It was me," he said, turning away from French.	266.4–9	When Silas finally tells the truth about what happened in 1982, French is pushing Larry to admit his guilt. The description here of how Silas feels in the moment he decides to speak up reveals the intensity and pressure of his guilty secret.
[The cabin]	–	The cabin is the place of secrets. Alice and Silas are Carl's secret and he keeps them hidden there. Silas is Larry's secret, and they meet near the cabin to keep their friendship secret. Wallace hides Tina's body there: his secret is buried in the floor of the cabin. The cabin is also the focus for Wallace's secret fantasies, things he can only share with "Scary Larry". The cabin in the woods, a familiar and much-used image from horror cinema, is the site of the darkest secrets in the story: a secret place itself, known to "but a handful of people in the world" (259.21), a place so lost and secret that it has already been reclaimed by the forests when Silas finally finds it and discovers Tina's grave.

3.5 Themes

TEXT	PP.	ANALYSIS
		As a projection surface for Wallace's murderous fantasies it is also a focus for very dark, private secrets, making it even more a secret, which is better left hidden, better forgotten and allowed to be reclaimed by the forest.

Guilt, responsibility and betrayal

Fight between Larry and Silas

There is a lot of guilt to be shared around in the novel. There is betrayal and bad behaviour and many things are said and done for reasons which are not always good. Two majorly significant examples – for the plot and the themes of the novel and for the characters themselves – are the **fight** between Larry and Silas in 1979 in which Larry calls him "n****r" (pp. 116–120), and Silas' continued silence concerning what he knows about **the night Cindy Walker disappeared** in 1982.

Both Carl Ott and Wallace Stringfellow are guilty: Wallace of the most terrible crimes and Carl of having been unfaithful to his wife and turned his two sons against one another by making them fight.

Responsibility

The theme of responsibility is closely associated with **the theme of guilt** in *Crooked Letter*. Silas' development as a character is all about him accepting responsibility for the damage he has caused Larry. The conclusion of the story is not the identification of Wallace as Tina's killer: it is Silas and Larry's reconciliation following Silas' confession and acknowledgment of his guilt and responsibility.

3.5 Themes

TEXT	PP.	ANALYSIS
[Larry's phone calls to Silas]	42–43	Silas rejects Larry here, ignoring the first answering machine message and rudely getting rid of Larry on the second call. There is barely a whisper of Silas' guilt in this early passage – "remembering … what Silas had done, how he'd beaten Larry when Larry said what he said" (43.18–20) – and that whisper is justified by what "Larry said".
Look at you, 32 Jones, he thought. You done ignored the poor fucker all this time and now all the sudden you care?	46.12–13	The circumstances surrounding Tina Rutherford's disappearance have made several people remember "Scary Larry". Silas notices that Larry is not at his repair shop and begins to wonder whether something has happened to him. But we can see in hindsight, having read the story, that there is more to Silas' concern here than simply a police officer's instincts: although still unable to confront or articulate it, deep inside Silas knows that he is connected to Larry's status as an outsider. His interest in the case has a cause and a motivation – his guilt and responsibility – which he is unable to acknowledge.
…relieved not to have to go see Larry.	83.25–26	Silas' guilty conscience is evident early on in the story, but only takes shape and becomes clear as time passes. Its shadowy forms early on, like in this passage, show that Silas has effectively hidden his guilt from himself until it has become something he never identifies or looks at directly.

3.5 Themes

TEXT	PP.	ANALYSIS
In the closet, behind his two extra uniforms, where he wouldn't have to look at it, was the Marlin lever-action .22 rifle.	96.22–23	Silas still has the gun Larry gave him and which he "won" in the fight. But the operative phrase here is "wouldn't have to look at it". Silas' suppressed guilt is explicitly symbolised here by Silas hiding the object at the heart of the fight with Larry. The fact that he still has it, after 25 years, is also deeply significant: no matter how much he ignores Larry and buries his own guilt, Silas is unable to leave the past behind him.
Silas looked out the window at the mill's smokestacks, relieved again not to have to face Larry. For so long he'd used that stuttered "nigger" as an excuse to avoid him. … Silas had never asked about Larry […] Scary Larry they'd begun to call him […]. … Silas would change the subject, put Larry out of his mind.	121.11–18	Silas feels guilty about Larry and knows that he is avoiding the man and his own guilt. This short passage illustrates how he avoids both. The progression of his awareness of his guilt can be seen here, as there is a little more detail and a little more shape to the issue than in the previously quoted example.
He longed to … mow his way back to the boy he'd been and do it differently with Larry, go to the police and say, "She was with me."	251.4–11	Silas begins to acknowledge his culpability and the guilt he feels. He regrets deeply having turned his back on Larry – using the racial insult as an excuse – and is no longer able to avoid the consequences of his actions.
"Why," Larry asked, "would he do all that?"	258.3	French has told Larry how Silas has been taking care of the chickens and looking after his property. Larry is puzzled: but the reader can see in

3.5 Themes

TEXT	PP.	ANALYSIS
		this brief moment how Silas' guilt is wearing him down, forcing him ever closer to confession and atonement.
"Is there something you want to say, then?" French asked. Here it all came. A quarter of a century bunching up on him, bearing down, a truck slamming on its brakes and its logs sliding forward, over the cab, through the window, the back of his head, shooting past him on the road. "It was me," he said, turning away from French.	266.4–9	This is the moment when Silas finally decides to tell the truth about what happened. He feels the pressure of his guilt and his responsibility and expresses it in a powerful and striking image.
"The thing," Larry said, "that I wanted to tell you that first time … was that I was sorry. About what I said, when Daddy made us fight."	271.28–30	Larry's guilt seems like a very small thing when compared to Silas', but it has obviously been bothering him for years, and he had made the effort to reach out to Silas to apologise. But Silas, motivated by his own suppressed guilt, had ignored and rejected the effort.
"Guilt," he said. […] "Well, sugar," she said, limping off, "don't be too hard on yourself. Now and again it's okay to let yourself off the hook." But that was his trouble, wasn't it? Letting himself off the hook had been his way of life.	287.13–21	This key passage shows accepting responsibility. Silas is moving step by step towards acceptance, confession and redemption, but he is struggling with every step. Having confessed the truth to Larry and to Roy French, he now feels that he must make things right – redeem himself.

3.5 Themes

TEXT	PP.	ANALYSIS
[Cindy and Larry]	Chapter 7, 145–173	One of the most significant chapters in the book, Chapter 7, contains the truth about the night in 1982 when Cindy went missing. This is essentially a story of betrayal and guilt: Cindy betrays Larry by manipulating him and exploiting his loneliness and infatuation, and Silas betrays Larry by allowing him to take the blame for something of which he was completely innocent. When Larry is talking to her at school (pp.149-150) he doesn't notice that while he is telling her what film they'll be going to see – *The Amityville Horror* – she is not paying attention to him, but is instead "looking toward the baseball field" (149.12) where Silas is practising with M&M. She acts "embarrassed" (151.12) when he tries to get her attention at school during the week before their supposed date. Larry sees none of these warning signs and walks right into a situation, which will destroy his life.
His elbow ached all the time, but he'd decided to stop taking the Lortabs. He didn't fool himself: the pain was penance. Were his visits to Mrs. Ott more penance?	313.6–9	Penance is an act that you give yourself to do in order to show that you are sorry for something you have done. Silas is punishing himself to show that he is sorry for what he has done to Larry.

3.5 Themes

Power

Below are some examples and discussions of the different kinds of power-based relationships in the novel.

Larry and Silas:
Passive and active agents, powerlessness and power

Despite being the central character, **Larry is utterly powerless**. He is beaten back and forth by events from the beginning, and at no point can he take control of his own life. As a child he is dominated by his father, by his loneliness and related need to make contact, to have friends. He is absolutely powerless in the face of the suspicion that he has killed Cindy Walker. After withdrawing into **hermit-like isolation** as an adult, he is shot by Wallace and spends the present-day time frame of the novel **in a coma**. In the present day Larry is powerless, and is the passive focus of the plot: he is being investigated. It is Silas who is active, Silas who investigates.

Larry: No control

When Larry is transferred from his military training to Jackson, Mississippi, "this new part of his life [seemed] not so much like another chapter in a novel as a different dream in the same night's sleep" (p. 172.20–22). This evocative phrase perfectly summarises the powerlessness and unreality of poor Larry's life from his lonely childhood to his ostracised, outsider adulthood.

Silas has more power. He is an **active agent** in the plot, and as a law enforcement officer and a popular and charming man he has a greater diversity of interaction with the other characters and their environment. He investigates the mystery surrounding Larry's being shot. He uses his initiative to actively pursue hunches and clues and evidence. He has a relationship with an equally strong-minded person (Angie) and, as the story progresses and he learns more about his own past and Larry's, he is finally forced to actively

Silas: powerful

confront his own role in what has become of Larry – the damage caused by his power over Larry.

Silas also has a degree of power in the past, both explicitly as an outstanding athlete and as the winner when Carl Ott forces them to fight, and implicitly in the power he holds over Larry following the events of 1982.

Larry and Wallace: Power and fantasy

Obsessed with "Scary Larry"

A very significant comment made by Wallace highlights his own bizarre attitude towards power. He tells Larry, when talking about the cabin in the woods, "I used to imagine you'd find me playing in there and tie me up and keep me prisoner. But instead of killing me you'd just keep me out there and we'd get to be friends." (p. 218.22–25) This extraordinary fantasy – told by Wallace as an adult, but originating in his youth – draws attention to his emotional connection to abduction fantasies and relationships of power. He believed at the time he fantasised about this that Larry was truly "Scary Larry", the murderer of Cindy Walker. So he actually **wanted to be taken prisoner by a dangerous killer**, to be "kept" by such a man and to establish a deep relationship with him.

Wallace has been obsessed with Larry since he first heard about him when he was at school (see pp. 210–214). It would not be fair to say that Larry has any power over Wallace: it's really not Larry Ott with whom Wallace is obsessed. His obsession is with "Scary Larry" – a fantasy figure, a Frankenstein's monster built from local legend and his own, **personal fantasies**. What does actually have power over Wallace is his own imagination, the intensity and darkness of his own murderous sexual fantasy.

Withholding attention and acceptance as power

Many examples

Carl can make Cecil Walker do stupid things because the brutish

3.5 Themes

Cecil enjoys **getting attention** from a man he idolises. Carl makes Larry's life miserable and even lonelier by treating him with distance, coldness, contempt and eventually almost completely ignoring him. Ken and David can make Larry do stupid things because they know – even if it's doubtful whether these two boys could articulate the idea – that **he is lonely** and desperate for attention and a sense of belonging. Cindy can make Larry do what she wants because she also understands how weak and desperate he is due to his loneliness and, in her case, his infatuation. She sees him as a helpless, harmless tool. Alice Jones punishes Silas by withholding love and attention, even making her 13-year-old son sit at another table in the diner and forbidding him to talk to her. Silas punishes Larry by ignoring him – for decades.

All of the above are examples of how withholding attention, love, acceptance or inclusion can be used as a way to exert power. This **theme is deep and constant in the book**, touching on almost all of the other themes and ideas. Encounters between equals are rare.

Voyeurism, knowledge and power

There is an element of power to voyeurism and spying: to see without being seen. Both Larry and Wallace are voyeurs. Larry enjoys secretly watching Cindy Walker sunbathing (pp. 68.8–26, 111.5, 104–105). Wallace, as a boy, secretly sneaks into Larry's barn to indulge his curiosity about "Scary Larry". Wallace has been closely observing Larry for a while, his interest fed by his unhealthy fascination with his own fantasies about abduction, rape and murder.

Voyeurism and spying

Related to this is the **idea of knowledge** as power. Silas has enormously powerful, indeed life-changing, knowledge of Larry, which he refuses to use to good purpose. Silas knows that Larry was not responsible for the disappearance of Cindy Walker, and this knowledge could have saved Larry from a quarter-century of

Knowledge

3.5   Themes

ostracism, hatred and fear. Wallace has a degree of power over Larry, which is related to knowledge: Wallace knows more about Larry than Larry knows about him. While Wallace's assumption that Larry killed Cindy is incorrect, Larry has no clue that Wallace is behind the disappearance of Tina Rutherford. This knowledge is of course closely related to Wallace having spied on Larry over the years.

Authority, violence and power

Human abuse of power

Power can be subtle (as seen in the voyeurism of Larry and Wallace) and it can also be **brutally** explicit, in the form of violence. The most extreme example of this kind of power is of course **Wallace's rape and murder** of Tina Rutherford – murder being the single most extreme and final form of power being abused. But before we reach this outer limit of human abuse of power, there are other examples. Cecil's physical abuse of Larry and the menacing, sexually charged violence with which he threatens Cindy are brutish, physical expressions of power. Carl Ott's authority as a father and husband has a similarly menacing edge of brute force about it: he is a physically powerful and dominating figure. Carl's sadism is a complex and insidious example of power and its abuses.

The nature of authority is that it has power over others: fathers have power over their children and people in uniforms have power over civilians. Silas and Roy French and Sheriff Lolly have power over Larry and others because they represent the authority – the power – of the state, of society itself.

Family affairs

The authority of parents, fathers (specifically Carl Ott) and mothers (specifically Alice Jones), provides examples of intimate and complex power structures. Larry submits to Carl's power – he is quite simply afraid of his father, and his longing for love and recognition has been almost completely crushed by his father's contempt.

3.5 Themes

Silas on the other hand is much more active in the struggle for power with his mother, despite secretly understanding why she is so stern with him.

Ina Ott, alone and afflicted by Alzheimer's disease, is increasingly powerless. She is at the mercy of the callous staff in the nursing home where she lives. The people who work there treat her like an annoying chore, a job they have to do but can't be bothered to do properly. When Silas visits her (pp. 235–239) he finds her in a terribly neglected state, lying in her own faeces because no one has come to help her or clean her up. She is a victim here not of the abuse of power, but of neglect by those around her when she herself has no power to help herself.

Belonging

> "But after a while, after I'd got me that rifle from Larry, and after I started playing baseball, I felt like I belonged here. It's part of why I came back, after all this time." (Silas, p. 178.4–6)

Belonging, in all its many aspects and forms, is a central theme in the novel. The nature of belonging is constantly questioned, most obviously in the two central characters and their role-reversals: Larry, born and bred in Chabot, tied to the land, and Silas, imported at age 13 from Chicago. But by the present day Larry is an unwelcome outsider, a hermit, no longer belonging to the community, whereas Silas has become a popular local figure, known to everyone and well-liked. He completely belongs to the community, to the extent that he is a figure of authority (a law enforcement officer) and is affectionately known by most people simply as "32". We see here with these two characters and their shifting degrees of belonging how fluid the concept itself is. Belonging is deeply ambiguous: it

Ambiguous

3.5 Themes

can provide **comfort as well as creating a kind of prison**. It can substitute for family – or it can represent an unwelcome last resort, as is the case for Alice when she leaves Chicago and fails to find a home for herself and Silas on the way South. She didn't want to have to return to Chabot and Fulsom: but her lack of options and her great need drive her back there.

Social community

Characters belong (or not) to the community in its wider sense, as well as to smaller units like racial groups, social classes, families or groups of friends – or even a two-person relationship, as is the case with Wallace and Larry, whose unlikely friendship allows both of these weird outsiders to find, however temporarily, a place to "belong". The fact of not belonging – of being ostracised – powers the dominant emotional theme in the novel, which is Larry's loneliness.

Feeling like you belong nowhere: loneliness

> "I don't know anybody except my momma and she don't know me." (Larry p. 261.26–27)

Friendship and family

The theme of loneliness is huge in the novel, and it encompasses related issues such as friendship and family. It is of course most directly relevant to Larry Ott, who as a boy was so lonely that his mother prayed for him **to find a friend**, and whose loneliness by adulthood has become so deep and constant that he befriends the weird and creepy Wallace Stringfellow, just so he can have **someone to talk to**. It is also relevant to Alice Jones, a woman whom circumstance has forced to be alone, against her nature and personality.

3.5 Themes

TEXT	PP.	ANALYSIS
"Lord," she would pray, "thank You for Your grace. Please help Larry read good tomorrow … and send him a special friend, Lord, one just for him." … And then Silas had come. A friend.	114.19–27	Larry's mother prays for him every night when he is young, asking God to send him a special friend. These prayers are still repeated after he has met Silas, because he keeps that friendship secret from her. The loneliness he feels as a child worries his mother: she sees that he has no friends, that he is alone at school.
Having a black friend was an interesting idea … Other white boys would speak to him on occasion, usually if they were alone with him … Larry hurried through the halls … the new kid who was never quite accepted …	69.8-25	School life is divided along racial lines. Larry had never considered befriending a black kid until he met Silas. He is not accepted by white kids, so he has nothing to lose here. All he wants is a friend: his loneliness drives him.
Ken and David	69–75	Here is one of Larry's most shameful memories, as he lowers himself in his desperate loneliness to go along with Ken and David's racist foolishness. The two boys manipulate Larry – like Cindy will three years later – and he suffers for it.
Larry's vehicle was the most cared-for in the county, a patient with its own full-time doctor. Larry riding along, ear cocked for any rattle, hoping for a knock, a belt to squeal, the brakes to whine.	124.4–7	Loneliness makes Larry desperate for distractions. He has no friends, no social life, his business is dead because of his notoriety, and he has nothing to fill his time with apart from "hoping" for something to go wrong with his car.

3.5 Themes

TEXT	PP.	ANALYSIS
Larry looked at the corn on his tray, too happy to eat, a date the next day and friends to tell about it.	152.27–29	It is March 1982: Larry thinks he is going on a date with Cindy and believes that afterwards he will have a group of friends – Ken, David, Philip, others – to talk with about it. The prospect alone makes him "too happy to eat" – a poignant illustration of his terrible loneliness. He cannot suspect that what is to come will destroy his life forever and that he will lose all hope of ever finding friendship and escaping his loneliness.
"How would you characterize your relationship with him?" French asked. "With Wallace Stringfellow?" "I thought he was my friend." "You got a strange taste in friends." "I don't know if you noticed," Larry said, "but I ain't had a lot of options." … "Yeah, well. Can you tell me about him?" … "We were both lonesome," he said. "I think that's why he came to see me in the first place."	299.3–23	Being questioned by Roy French after waking from the coma, Larry is quite candid about his loneliness and lack of friends. He also displays the empathy and generosity of spirit that lies beneath his loneliness again: Larry is not a judgmental man. He knows that Wallace is a weirdo and an outcast, but he has lived himself as a pariah for 25 years.

3.5 Themes

TEXT	PP.	ANALYSIS
Until you ate you didn't know how hungry you were, how empty you'd become. Wallace's visits had shown him that being lonesome was its own fast, that after going unnourished for so long, even the foulest bite could remind your body how much it needed to eat. That you could be starving and not even know it.	222.28– 223.18	In this profound and poignant insight, Larry compares loneliness to religious fasting, something he had become familiar with when his mother started attending a new church after the disappearance of Cindy Walker. He follows this insight by praying for God to "help Wallace, God. Please."
He'd refused to see the truth, that she was starving from loneliness.	192.24–25	Silas has a difficult relationship with his mother. He punishes her with coldness and blames her for the course their lives take when they leave Chicago. He continues to blame her for trying to keep him from Cindy Walker. But despite all his anger and resentment, he does at some level understand that his mother is desperately lonely – as lonely in her own way as Larry is. And it is worth paying attention here to the linking of eating and nourishment with loneliness: as in the example above in which Larry compares loneliness to religious fasting.

Loneliness and belonging: the Halloween party

An extremely important episode in the history of Larry's loneliness and desire to belong is the Halloween story Silas tells to Angie (pp. 178–181). Larry's hyper-realistic zombie mask (see the section

Zombie mask

3.5 Themes

on Horror and monsters below for more on the mask) is, ironically, the key to a brief moment of true belonging and **popularity for him** at school. The kids "flocked around him" and "pretty girls, cheerleaders, passed it head to head trying it on". He is invited to be a part of a Halloween party. He has his "own room" at the party house, a room full of excited and thrilled visitors, where he in his mask is constantly surrounded by other people. After the party he expects to be included in the party and accepted by the group outside, to which Cindy and Silas belong: but "we all just kind of pretended not to see him. All of us." (p. 179.32) Silas had been watching Larry all night, closely observing how excited he was to be a **part of society** and to actually belong among other people. He could see and he could understand how important this was to Larry, how much pleasure it must have given him: and he (and Cindy and all the other "cool kids" outside the Haunted House) still goes out of his way to ignore Larry and reinforce his outsider status, his otherness – **his lack of belonging**.

Foreshadowing of adulthood

This episode is an important foreshadowing of Larry's life post Cindy Walker: here, he is accepted and can **belong while he is wearing a mask**, but as soon as the mask is off, he is ostracised, driven away, forced to become the outsider again. This is the entirety of his adult life for 25 years after the disappearance of Cindy Walker – only then, he does not choose to put the mask on himself, he is instead given a mask to wear, that of "Scary Larry", by everyone else. He is forced out of the warm circle of belonging and **made a monster**, an outsider.

Silas also recalls this night: lying in hospital after the showdown with Wallace, Silas watches Larry in the next hospital bed and remembers the Halloween party, wondering what would have been different if he had not turned his back on Larry that night, if he had asked him to stay. As Silas understands it, 25 years later, Larry's life

3.5 Themes

might in a way have been saved by that small gesture of kindness and forgiveness (p. 302.20–24).

Belonging to a family: fathers, mothers, sons and brothers

Family bonds are at the heart of *Crooked Letter* – the two main characters are, unknown to each other, half-brothers. Carl Ott looms large as a presence even after his death, and the fight he causes between the two boys shapes their lives and is the root of the entire story. **Silas feels the lack of a father** when he was growing up acutely. His relationship with his mother Alice is also complex, and continues to occupy him after she has died.

The Ott family

TEXT	PP.	ANALYSIS
One photo at the bottom showed baby Larry in a woman's lap … A maid, he thought … Only one photo showed her face … this woman was his mother.	130.21–29	When Silas is searching through Larry's house he finds old photographs and discovers the truth of his history.
[Alice and Silas leave Chicago and travel south to Mississippi]	131–143, 192	Silas' memories of the move from Chicago to Chabot when he was 13 provide the most comprehensive insight we have into his relationship with his mother. We see here how she was hard to begin with, and becomes harder the further south they go: we can also see here how Silas understands, even as a young boy, how men find his mother attractive and how she uses that to get by in life. In contrast to Ina Ott, who surrounds Larry with as much comfort, love and support as she can, Alice tries to raise her son by instilling in him a sense of strength, self-reliance and the hardness of the world.

3.5 Themes

TEXT	PP.	ANALYSIS
[Silas visits Ina Ott in the nursing home]	184–185, 235–239	Silas visits Larry's mother in the nursing home more than once. The first visit is a waste of his time: Ina Ott is unable to concentrate or re-member. The next time he visits he has to organise care for the helpless old woman, who is lying in soiled clothes and is very distressed. He is able to talk to her this time, and she remembers Alice and remembers also that Silas and Larry had been friends. But Silas' questions make her afraid: there is something in the past she can't or won't remember and which frightens her.
He understood that Carl liked most everyone except him.	61.25	Here are three examples illustrating how poor Larry's relationship with his father is. He knows that he is a disappointment and that his father actually doesn't like him and has no way to communicate with him. The third example here shows how sad the situation is for a young boy: he doesn't know what it is to be happy with his father.
… uncomfortable be-cause he and his father almost never touched …	56.28–29	
… Larry, hidden, listen-ing, the stories weaving his imagination and the sounds of his father's voice into what must have been happiness …	66.27–28	

3.5 Themes

TEXT	PP.	ANALYSIS
[The fight]	116–120	This pivotal scene is the original crisis from which the plot of the story rises – everything begins here. Carl's cruelty pits his two sons against one another, and the insult (from Larry) and beating (from Silas) destroy their friendship. Carl causes humiliation in Larry and shame in Silas, bringing out the very worst in both boys.
… Silas fighting to get away, nearly crying himself as he said, "Let me go, Mr. Ott, please," and Carl slurring something in his ear that made Silas bat his hands away. He broke free and sprinted toward the far woods and Larry was left alone, on the ground, in the weeds, with his father.	120.17–23	This is the end of the scene where Carl forces the boys to fight, and it is a good symbolic summary of their family constellation – Carl and his two sons. Larry is defeated and helpless on the ground, stuck with Carl, and Silas has fought free and run away.
"You've never minded," Larry's mother said to Alice, looking hard at her, "using other people's things."	60–61	Larry is only a young boy when he witnesses the brief and cold confrontation between his mother and Alice Jones. The truth will come out later: Ina Ott sees her former maid as having been a "loose" woman, and knows that her husband was unfaithful with her. The coats she gives Alice for herself and Silas represent a humiliating act of insufficient pity and contempt.

3.5 Themes

TEXT	PP.	ANALYSIS
Cecil leaned over and nudged Carl and reached out and tugged at Cindy's towel. She slapped Cecil's hand but he held on and pulled harder …	109.8– 110.13	Larry and Silas see Cecil harassing Cindy. There is a combination here of Cecil's typical showing off in front of Carl, but also his unhealthy interest in his step-daughter. We can see in Cecil's sadistic and abusive sexuality a foreshadowing of Wallace Stringfellow, and in the friendship between Cecil and Carl a very dark foreshadowing of the friendship between another white trash outsider (Wallace) and Carl Ott's son.
That night, as she had every night of his life, his mother came into his room and sat on his bed … During his attacks of asthma, she'd stayed up with him as he struggled to breathe … she'd prayed the stuttering would go away … "…and send him a special friend, Lord, one just for him."	113.28– 115.18	Ina Ott's devotion to Larry is in contrast to Alice Jones' much harder attitude to Silas. Larry and his mother are devoted to one another, and when she is old and suffering from Alzheimer's in a nursing home, he tries to see her as often as he can, hoping to be there on the rare days when her mental state lets her hold conversations and remember who he is.
He had felt, at that moment, most acutely in his life, the absence of a father … He started to run, afraid not of the darkness coming, but of the anger scratching at his ribs.	189.13–14	Larry had shown Silas how to use the lawn mower, and Silas had cut the grass at the Ott house. But when Carl returns it is Larry who gets the praise. Silas' anger at resentment at what he sees as Larry having more than him contributes to the intensity of his feelings when their friendship is broken.

3.5 Themes

TEXT	PP.	ANALYSIS
A lot of people came, he knew, to see him, the sense he was going places, even old Carl Ott sometimes.	244.32–33	Carl comes to watch Silas play, a brief hint again of the truth of their relationship: and a reminder that, as Larry says, Silas is the son Carl would rather have had – athletic, strong, successful, popular.
"He wished you'd been the white one," Larry said.	304.29	Speaking to Silas about Carl, Larry identifies the truth. He had always been a disappointment to his father. Larry is much closer to his mother's side of the family (see p. 62), while Silas has inherited Carl's physicality and forceful, at times even cold, nature.
"My little doppelgänger," Colin said.	62.25–34	This awkward scene from Larry's childhood highlights how much closer he is in nature and physical type to his mother's side of the family, here specifically his uncle Colin. Carl is disgusted and baffled by the more urbane, sensitive Colin, treating him like a "crime against nature" (p. 62.13).
"We're brothers," he said. "Half brothers." "Did you know?" "No," Larry said, then, "Yeah. Ever since yall got in our truck that morning, I knew something. Then when Momma give yall them coats…" … "You think it was better," Larry said, "living with him?"	304.20–305.15	Larry was an observant and intelligent child, and he understood why the strange confrontation between Alice and Ina over the coats was so intense. In this scene at the hospital, Silas and Larry also talk about Carl, their father. There is a definite ambiguity here to their feelings. Larry suffered under Carl's contempt and coldness, and while Silas understands what a bad man and bad father Carl Ott had been, as a boy he felt the acute pain of not having had a father.

3.5   Themes

TEXT	PP.	ANALYSIS
… "No," Silas admitted … "It wasn't easy without one, either. I used to wish I was you…"		As Larry points out about fasting and loneliness, and how when you're hungry even the "foulest bite" tastes good, Silas has such a hunger for a father that he even envies Larry having Carl, a cruel man who forced his sons to fight one another and cheated on his wife with their maid.

Finding a sense of belonging in friendship

> "You got a strange taste in friends."
> "I don't know if you noticed," Larry said, "but I ain't had a lot of options." (Roy French and Larry Ott, p. 299.6–8)

The issue of friendship is as ambiguous and untidy as are the other themes of belonging which are addressed in the book. The ideal of friendship is **tainted by secrets, exploitation, desperation** and unhealthy interests.

TEXT	PP.	ANALYSIS
"…send him a special friend, Lord, one just for him…"	114.22	Larry's loneliness has a desperate, grasping aspect when he is a child. His mother prays for God to send him a friend.
[Larry insults a black girl at school to impress Ken and David]	69.26– 75.32	He wants friends. He wants to be among other people and to have relationships with them. This leads him to debase himself by racially insulting black girls at school in an effort to ingratiate himself with two white boys. The situation is horrible, and Larry not only gets in trouble with a teacher and then gets beaten up by

3.5 Themes

TEXT	PP.	ANALYSIS
		another black girl in front of the class: "Even today, more than a year later … the memory shamed him" (p. 76.1–2).
"Because Silas had started playing baseball at school, Larry worried that he was losing him."	104.7–8	The desperation is also very apparent when it comes to his friendship with Silas.
…too happy to eat…	152.28	A brief moment of acceptance and belonging to a group of white kids at school.
"Why you want to talk to him?" "Cause we used to be friends." "He mentioned something about that, but didn't sound like yall was friends. More like you just went to the same school." "We were friends," Larry said. "Okay. We all remember things different, I guess."	259.10–15	Larry's need for friendship means that he sees relationships less clearly than others: he is easily deceived. When he wakes from his coma and is being interviewed by French and Lolly, he says again and again that he and Silas were friends when they were kids. French is sceptical.
"We were friends. Weren't we, Silas?" "You were, Larry … I don't know what I was."	268.4–7	After Silas' confession about the night Cindy went missing in 1982, the nature of their friendship and Silas' betrayal of it becomes a painful topic for the two men.
…he'd felt a kind of protection for the man who'd shot him. Who'd been his friend … But he'd thought Silas had been his friend, too, hadn't he? Maybe Larry was wrong about the word friend…	283.26–284.2	Later, Larry comes to despair of the idea of friendship. He has decided to tell Roy French everything he knows about Wallace, as he is now convinced that it was Wallace who had killed Tina Rutherford and shot him. The revelation of Silas' betrayal – which had pretty much ruined his

3.5 Themes

TEXT	PP.	ANALYSIS
		entire life – is combined with his acceptance of what Wallace has done. The only two "friends" Larry has ever had have both betrayed him, in different ways, and both have destroyed his life, again in very different ways – Silas by hiding the truth, Wallace by shooting and framing him for the murder of Tina Rutherford.

Belonging to a community: Acceptance and ostracism

Larry said, "I just wanted to, you know, say welcome back. To the crooked letter." (p. 43.15–16)

Rural Mississippi

The novel is about a specific place (this is already evident in the title) and features constant interaction between the characters and the landscape: Larry afflicts the town like a contamination and in turn the land swallows up the old cabin in the woods. Larry's ostracism is a constant throughout the novel, enhancing the ambiguity of belonging by showing a man who has spent his entire life in this place, is deeply **rooted in the traditions** and knowledge of country life, and is at the same time an outcast, utterly isolated.

3.5 Themes

TEXT	PP.	ANALYSIS
Had Larry caused this section of town to dry up?	123.28–29	The presence of Ottomotive Repair is like an infection: Larry's ostracism includes a fear of contamination by association or proximity.
[Alice and Silas leave Chicago for the South]	131–143	Alice and Silas leave Chicago and head south. The world becomes increasingly strange to Silas: He finds everything weird and different. He grew up in Chicago, in the north, and the south is for him another world. Silas grew up until the age of 13 in a place where he felt he belonged, where he had no doubt about his belonging: in a black neighbourhood in Chicago. It is only once he and his mother begin to head south, first to Tennessee and then to Mississippi, that he feels like an outsider. There is an irony here in that he is originally from Mississippi, the son of Carl Ott, and that he is literally returning to his first home. This irony is an important aspect of the ambiguity of belonging in the novel.
Because of Larry's past the women who shared her room were always the furthest gone, those who wouldn't be aware that a perhaps-murderer visited, those with no family, no one to complain.	196.30–33	Larry's mother in the nursing home is also affected – even if she may not realise it – by her son's notoriety. Only the most far-gone patients share a room with her, those who won't be aware that a "perhaps-murderer" occasionally visits. Larry's status even impacts his mother in her nursing home.

3.5   Themes

TEXT	PP.	ANALYSIS
"You from Chicago?" He said he was. "What's it like up there?" …He told her how the snow sometimes covered cars entirely … freezing Lake Michigan glittering under the lights … Chicago pizza was the best…	242.31– 243.24	Silas remembers Chicago, telling Cindy about it. He obviously belonged there: It was his home, where he grew up, and he has been shaped by the cold, huge city to the north. Chabot is an alien world for him: He doesn't belong here.

Belonging to the land: Larry teaches Silas about nature
Larry's extensive knowledge of nature and the traditions of living close to plants and animals is a constant source of wonder to Silas. Larry teachers Silas a lot about rural life, including how to shoot guns and mow lawns, and Silas continues to remember these lessons even 25 years later. Larry also teaches Silas other things, explains what words mean, and introduces him to books and stories by telling him his favourite Stephen King stories.

Belonging to society: class and status

Cindy and Tina

An important distinction is made between the two female victims of the crimes in the story, and this distinction is one of class – specifically, **wealth and status**. Cindy Walker's stepfather is a deadbeat, an unemployed alcoholic with no self-respect, no money, no job and no prospects. Tina Rutherford on the other hand is the daughter of the most powerful and wealthiest family in the district, owners of vast areas of woodland, and apparently the most important employer in an area with little in the way of work or opportunities.

Symmetries

As with so many of the themes and events in the novel, these two girls represent a **lopsided symmetry**. Reflecting their origins, their stories end differently: Tina, the wealthy princess, is discovered (her

3.5 Themes

body is found) and avenged. When she is buried the mill shuts down for the day – the whole town shuts down, Silas notes (226.16–17). Cindy however, publicly shamed as a "slut" (p. 152.12) and a "little whore" (p. 160.3), is lost forever. Her body is never found. Her presumed killer is never identified. The truth about what happened to her can never be known. No one is left to care or grieve for her. There is a sad continuation of the differences in their status and their "value" to society even after their deaths.

Another example of the **class differences** in the community is seen when Silas attends (from a distance) Tina Rutherford's funeral and compares her grave with the place where his mother is buried (pp. 226.29–227.5).

There is also an obvious difference in class and status between Larry Ott and Wallace Stringfellow. Larry comes from a land-owning family and was raised to be polite and respectful. His mother was a loving and caring presence, and his father, although he was cold, unfaithful to his wife, cruel to the point of sadism and eventually rejected his son completely, provided a model of sorts by maintaining routines and working hard for a living. Wallace on the other hand is barely able to form complete, functioning sentences, speaking mostly in a mangled form of English which is more like a dialect than an accent. He has very low standards when it comes to personal hygiene and personal grooming. His general behaviour – his pushy, invasive approach and his shifty vibe – contrasts with Larry's polite, well-mannered and reserved attitude. These are also aspects of the **two outsiders' very different personalities**, but the superficialities and the structures of their behaviour are rooted in their very different social backgrounds.

Larry and Wallace

We see more of the "white trash" culture in the area where **Irina** lives, which is also referred to as White Trash Avenue (p. 47.32), as well as in **the Walkers** – Cecil most definitely conforms to a white

"White trash"

1 FORWORD –
AT A GLANCE

2 TOM FRANKLIN:
LIFE & WORK

3 ANALYSES AND
INTERPRETATIONS

3.5 Themes

trash stereotype. **Ken and David**, the two boys who trick Larry into racially abusing a black girl at school, are "poorer than Larry – he knew this because they got free lunches" (p. 69.29–30), and their crude racism and behaviour mark them as another example of "white trash" in the novel.

> **White trash** refers to very poor whites, and is usually applied to those who live in the rural South. They have very low social status and a very poor standard of living. They are stereotypically – in mainstream culture – associated with gun culture, alcoholism and drug problems, domestic abuse, racism and a generally obnoxious kind of ignorance. It should be remembered that this term, while in common use, is abusive and insulting, and that the racial element to it is also problematic.

Race: Identity and taboos

The abusive racist term "n****r" is used throughout the book by white characters. Many characters use it casually, with no hostility or menace, but Larry knows how bad it is. The two times he uses the word **he is shocked at himself** for having said it. He seems to not just fear the consequences – getting beaten up by the black girl in class in 1979 was bad enough – but also to know how wrong it is, how **hurtful and nasty**. Twenty-five years later, he still wants to apologise to Silas.

3.5 Themes

TEXT	PP.	ANALYSIS
He was terrified of black kids.	58.2	School rezoning means Larry has to change schools, and he is surrounded by black kids who are bigger, faster and stronger than he is.
In Fulsom his father dropped the boys off at school, Alice climbing out and then Silas, Larry aware how unusual, inappropriate, it was for black people to be getting out of a white man's truck.	58.22–25	The division of the races is deeply embedded in society. Even young children are aware that black people and white people aren't supposed to interact in a personal way.
[Feeling intimidated by the black majority at school and isolated from the other white kids, Larry racially insults a black girl to impress Ken and David; he is then beaten up by another black girl in front of the class]	69.8–75.32	This shameful episode shows us a lot about racial divisions and dynamics in the school and society at large, but it also shows us that Larry's attempts to dabble in racism are a terrible mistake. He doesn't subscribe to the racist nonsense: He feels ashamed of having abused the girl. He knows it's wrong; he feels the wrongness, and his shame stems more from this sense of having done the wrong thing than from having been beaten up by a girl in public.
"Is it cause I'm white?" Larry asked. "What?" "Why your momma don't want you to play with me?"	102.16–18	Alice is concerned about interactions between the races (see below for her comments on Silas and Cindy), but while Larry is not wrong here, he has not touched on the truth, which is that Alice wants to minimise contact between herself and Silas and Carl Ott.

3.5 Themes

TEXT	PP.	ANALYSIS
The three of them lived on a quiet, all-black street in an all-black neighborhood … Silas had never even seen the projects, might as well have been Mars to him. But he hadn't seen many white people, either. It wasn't until he and his mother came south that he encountered them.	131.8–21	Silas' experiences with race and racism changed dramatically when he and his mother came south. He had been accustomed to living in a peaceful black community, and he only encounters white racism and antagonistic race relations down in Mississippi.
The smile she wore was the one she used around white people.	144.1–2	Silas sees how his mother adapts and changes her manner when interacting with white people. Being a child, he learns from this.
"Yo momma likes nig-gers," Larry said quietly. Before he'd thought.	152.16	Larry's desperate need for friends and attention still leads him to do and say stupid things which demean him. He automatically goes along with the type of comments the other white boys use, but he knows – "Before he'd thought" – that it's wrong.
…to the window where their trays were taken by thick black hands…	152.31	Compare this with the white lawyers referenced below: Black people are associated almost exclusively with menial labour.
…the white lawyers in suits walking down one side of the long concrete steps and the families of the black folks they would convict or acquit walking down the other.	174.4–6	Silas observes this: The racial divisions in this part of the country are very explicit here.

3.5 Themes

TEXT	PP.	ANALYSIS
"…his whole family poor as niggers…"	156.27	This is Carl Ott describing Cecil. The casual and contemptuous racism displayed by Carl signals how widespread and generally accepted these attitudes are in this society.
Silas noticed a dirty pillowcase stuffed back in the cage behind the seat and wondered should he look inside it. Wondered for a moment would it have eye holes, though in truth today's racism seemed less organized than when he'd been a boy.	191.9–13	Silas has stopped Wallace for trespassing and is examining his vehicle. This is a reference to the white sheets and hoods worn by the members of the white supremacist organisation the Ku Klux Klan (KKK). The KKK was particularly widespread in the south and remains a threatening force in the USA to this day, an aggressive and deep-rooted network of affiliated groups with a history of murderous racist violence and abuse.
"I got me a good [dog]. Part pit bull, part Chow? Name John Wayne Gacy? You ain't never seen a better watchdog. Hates niggers worse than anything." "How come?" "Just smart I guess. One ever comes up in the yard, he bout goes crazy. You ever want to borry him, say the word…" "That's all right. It ain't the black folks that messes with me."	206.19–27	As an adult, Larry's attitude towards black people has relaxed a great deal. Notice here how he no longer feels the need to go along with the crude racism of white people around him (Wallace in this case). Wallace's racism is as casual and natural to him as it was for Carl Ott, with an additional aggression and implied violence. Wallace represents a strain of white supremacy wherein very poor, socially disadvantaged whites attempt to maintain some degree of pride and identity by focussing their hatred and resentment on black people.

3.5 Themes

TEXT	PP.	ANALYSIS
Larry would wonder how many wrongs she'd endured from white people in her almost-century of living.	222.1–9	Larry's natural empathy comes out more when he is an adult and he has, to a degree, come to terms with his loneliness. He is less likely to mimic prevalent racist attitudes in order to conform. As an intelligent and naturally empathic person, he is fully aware of the damage and hurt racism has caused the black people around him.
…a graveyard miles out in the country, whites only buried there…	226.29–30	Segregation extends beyond death, with even graveyards being defined along racial lines.
"Son, nothing good ever come out of colors mixing."	246.24	Alice Jones speaking to Silas. What he doesn't know is that he is what comes out of "colors mixing". She is trying to warn him to stay away from Cindy Walker, who is white, because she has already learned that people are beginning to notice the unusual and unwanted spectacle of a black boy hanging around with a white girl. We can assume from what we know of Alice that this warning is not malicious in nature. Rather, she has experienced first-hand the problems that interracial relationships can cause, and wants to spare her son similar struggles.

3.5   Themes

Horror and monsters – outsiders

"Larry Ott returned home and found a monster waiting in his house." (p. 17.2–3)

"Larry felt a strange forgiveness for him because all monsters were misunderstood." (p. 24.22–23)

"Horror, it ain't my thing. Too much of that in real life."

(Silas, p. 265.1–2)

Horror plays a role in *Crooked Letter*: It is present in the culture the characters consume (Stephen King novels, horror films) as well as in the imagery (the zombie mask, the cabin in the woods) and the events (the acts of Wallace Stringfellow). One major element through the history of horror as a genre is **the idea of the monster** – ranging from the implicit threat of the 'outsider' to the full-blown inhuman or supernatural menace. *Crooked Letter* also contains monsters.

History of horror

The monsters in the book are **rejects and outsiders**. They are two men whose natures – one withdrawn and desperately lonely, the other weird and creepy – make it hard for them to interact with others. While Larry is completely innocent of what he is believed to have done – he is a monster in reputation only, not in fact – Wallace is in fact a monster whose obsession with rape and murder has become active.

Larry and Wallace

The monsters: "Scary Larry"

Wallace himself is nervous about Larry: When Larry asks him why he used the DIRECTV truck the first time he came to visit instead of riding his 4-wheeler, Wallace says he was worried Larry might cut him up and bury him in the woods (p. 208.23–27). Wallace, himself a real monster, is apparently nervous of Larry's fearsome (and inaccurate) reputation as a monster.

Larry: reputation as a monster

3.5 Themes

Wallace talks about when he first heard of Larry, when he was at school and all the kids were talking about the "creepy fellow" who went to the same school, sat at the same desks (pp. 211.2–11 and 211.31–212.8).

Society made Larry a monster

But the truth about Larry is that he is not a monster and he never was. He wears **a mask to scare** young Wallace and to take part in a Halloween party. He reads **horror stories** because he likes the stories. Society makes him a monster by reputation and innuendo – **"Scary Larry" is another mask**, this time one he didn't choose to put on, one that is forced on him.

The monsters: Wallace

> "You don't like me much, do you [...] It's okay. Not many folks do. All thank I'm weird. Why I quit school, got tired of em making fun of me." (p. 204.25–29)

For the reader, Wallace is a weird and unpleasant character when we first meet him, and continues to be so through his friendship with Larry. But he is only fully exposed (see pp. 218–219) on the last night of their friendship, when he starts talking about the cabin and tells Larry his extraordinary childhood fantasy of being abducted and "kept" there by Larry. Wallace then begins to talk about his obsessions with rape and murder. **This marks the end of their friendship**, despite Wallace having invoked it with such intensity to show that even if Larry had killed Cindy, they'd still be friends. But Larry, who is not a real monster, is deeply disturbed by what Wallace is saying and asks him to leave. He is shocked to see that Wallace has become sexually aroused by his talk of rape.

3.5 Themes

Stephen King

The famous author of horror fiction Stephen King – one of the best-selling fiction authors of all time – figures very prominently in the book. He is **Larry's favourite author** and, when Larry tells Silas the stories, he becomes a favourite of Silas' too (see p. 103). Silas doesn't like to read but he enjoys having Larry tell him the stories. It is only much later, while he is guarding Larry in the hospital, that Silas begins "reading the stories he never had as a kid" (p. 28.25). But he still prefers the way Larry told him the stories to the stories themselves (p. 265.1–3).

Famous writer of horror fiction

Many of King's works are referenced in the novel, including *Salem's Lot* (a vampire takes over a small town), *The Shining* (a haunted hotel takes possession of the caretaker), *Night Shift* (a collection of short stories), *The Dead Zone* (about psychic powers) and *Cujo* (a rabid dog terrorises a mother and her young son). Individual short stories are also mentioned: *The Mangler* (p. 105.3–4) is one of their favourites, and when Larry and Silas are in the cabin together as boys, Larry tells Silas the story *Trucks*, reciting it from memory because they have no light in the cabin (p. 103.8–27). He also tells Silas the story of *The Mangler* and *Jerusalem's Lot*, the prequel to the novel *Salem's Lot*.

Famous books

Stephen King is by no means an unusual or remarkable choice of author to be referred to here. He has long been one of the most famous and popular authors in the world, and the late 70s-early 80s – the time of Larry's childhood as seen in the novel – marked a **high point in his popularity.**

King is notable for his portrayal of "normal" Americans confronted with **extraordinary situations**, usually supernatural horror. His characters are typically working class, white, and generally inhabit one of two fictional towns in the northern state of Maine called Castle Rock or Derry. As a writer he returns again and again to certain

Supernatural horror

3.5   Themes

themes throughout his career, including **childhood and adolescence**, the dangers of stupidity and bigotry, the nature of **community and family**, and the emergence of heroism in unremarkable people.

Horror films and serial killers

In addition to the repeated mention of Stephen King (and occasional other thriller authors) the book mentions **several films** which had been released and were running in cinemas around the time (late 1970s-early 1980s). Mentioning films by name serves a couple of purposes: The films may have a thematic relevance or contribute in some way to the atmosphere or tone of the novel. More specifically, however, they serve to anchor the story in a real place and time. Characters in *Crooked Letter* watch films at the drive-in cinema, which helps to define the sense of place which is so important to the novel: This is a slightly old-fashioned, simple rural society.

Drive-in cinemas

Drive-in cinemas are open-air cinemas with a screen positioned in front of a parking area where visitors park their cars in arranged spaces. Each space has access to a speaker through which visitors can hear the sound of the film. Drive-ins have always been a predominantly rural phenomenon, and were most popular and widespread in the 1950s and 1960s. For many Americans, drive-ins are relics of an older, lost age of US culture and are associated with the origins of teen-focused pop culture.

Films in *Crooked Letter*

The films themselves illustrate the period. They provide examples of what people were watching at the time – even if this is a couple of years late, as we can see from the release dates of some of the

3.5 Themes

films. The films position the story in a specific time, which further solidifies the sense of place (see the section earlier on "belonging") and helps to establish a solid and cohesive foundation upon which the story can unfold.

Many films are referred to in *Crooked Letter, Crooked Letter*, and many of them are horror films. The exceptions are:

→ *Animal House* (1978), a raunchy comedy from the makers of National Lampoon comedy magazine.
→ *The Long Riders* (1980), a Western by Walter Hill.
→ The science fiction classic *Star Wars* (1977).
→ *Smokey and the Bandit* (1977), an action comedy about truckers.
→ *How the Grinch Stole Christmas* (1966), based on the picture book by Dr. Seuss.
→ *A Christmas Story* (1983), which is described as Larry's "favorite holiday movie" (p. 215.5).

Horror films are either clearly mentioned by name or are more obliquely referenced. Direct mention is made, for example, of the following films: *Phantasm* (1979), *Dawn of the Dead* (1978), and *The Amityville Horror* (1979).

The two oblique references are interesting. In both instances, the main characters (in both cases serial killers) from two films are mentioned, but not the titles of the films. The two are the genius cannibal killer Hannibal Lecter, from Jonathan Demme's *The Silence of the Lambs* (1991), and Norman Bates, the disturbed young murderer in Alfred Hitchcock's *Psycho* (1960). The fact that almost everyone who hears those names immediately knows which films they come from signals the **deep and widespread pervasiveness of horror culture** in our mainstream culture. When Lecter is mentioned in the conversation between Angie and Silas (p. 176.11–18), she is using him as an example to suggest that maybe Larry is

Serial killer

3.5 Themes

himself a serial killer. These fictional monsters and their historical inspirations are relevant to the **figure of Wallace Stringfellow** in the novel. Wallace displays many of the early warning signs of a budding serial killer.

Serial killers are defined as murderers who kill at least three victims, for the purposes of personal (psychological, emotional or sexual) gratification, over an extended period of time with a so-called "cooling-off" period between murders. These three factors may differ in intensity or magnitude, with the number of victims varying greatly or the cooling-off periods extending sometimes for years, but taken as guidelines in combination with the deeply personal motivations, they serve to differentiate genuine serial killers – who remain an extremely rare phenomenon – from mass murderers (who kill multiple victims in a single event) or one-off killers.

Serial killers have been a hugely popular subject for fiction and cinema for many years. The uniquely weird threat they pose and their typical combination of inhuman depravity and human weakness provide an unusual and extreme insight into the very furthest reaches of what it means to be human, and they are a constantly fertile source of inspiration for stories in the crime, thriller or horror genres. The macabre and ghoulish subcultures which have developed surrounding real life killers are briefly commented on in *Crooked Letter*, when Silas suggests that the eggs laid by "Scary Larry's" chickens could be sold "on eBay ... Or one of them serial killer Web sites." (p. 228.11–12)

3.5 Themes

Another reference to serial killers in the novel is in the name of Wallace Stringfellow's dog, John Wayne Gacy (see Wallace Stringfellow's entry in the Characters chapter in this book for notes on Gacy).

Symbols of horror: The mask

TEXT	PP.	ANALYSIS
...Larry Ott returned home and found a monster waiting for him.	17.2–3	The mask is the monster which opens the novel. It is a monstrous image covering the very real monster beneath – Wallace.
He turned and saw the monster's face, knowing it immediately for the mask it was, that he'd owned since he was a kid, that his mother had hated, his father ridiculed, a gray zombie with bloody gashes and fuzzy patches of hair and one plastic eye that dangled from strands of gore.	23.18–24	Wallace is wearing the mask when he shoots Larry, and we see here the first description of it. Silas describes it again later (p. 178). The mask is a potent symbol throughout the novel and plays a role in a few pivotal moments in Larry's life: the near-fatal shooting, his first contact with Wallace and the Halloween party where he almost became a happy child.
[Larry's mask and the Halloween party]	178.24–181.21	This lengthy passage, told to Angie by Silas, describes the Halloween party and the role the mask plays in giving Larry the illusion of being a popular, normal child with friends and a place to belong.

3.5 Themes

TEXT	PP.	ANALYSIS
When he was thirty-one years old … Larry began to notice things amiss in the barn … he heard someone tromping over the dry dead leaves behind the barn. Larry … hid in a stall … He had his old zombie mask and he put it on … He let the boy get fully in … before he stepped out from behind the stall with his arms raised and his fingers claws and yelled "Argh!" …Larry … left the mask in its spot in his closet and went to work.	195.1– 196.23	Larry uses the mask to scare off the trespassing boy (Wallace). This is the last time we see the mask in the chronology of the story before Wallace uses it when he shoots Larry. There is again a symmetry here, with the mask being worn by the two "monsters" in the book – "Scary Larry" and Wallace – to scare one another. Larry's use is a warning and Wallace's is a murderous reflection of that old fright.
…you put on the mask so it wasn't you doing it … he remembered the mask and he remembered the gun, he seemed himself the man in the mask waiting by the door for his other self to come home … Mask Larry marching up to Face Larry, pushing the gun against his heart and the two Larrys merging to one with one heart …	260.26– 261.18	Under pressure from French and Lolly to confess to having killed Tina and shot himself, and still weakened from his injuries, the surgery and the drugs, Larry finds his thinking increasingly confused. The mask hides identity and allows the wearer the freedom to do things they otherwise wouldn't: Larry is confusing Wallace in the mask with himself, drawing alarming parallels between them, seeing Wallace (in the mask) as a version of himself, a truly dark reflection, a version of himself much closer to him than his real (half-) brother Silas could ever be. The confusion of identities in this passage is a key moment for understanding the symbolic value of the zombie mask, as well as for seeing deeper into the strange symmetry between Wallace and Larry.

3.5 Themes

TEXT	PP.	ANALYSIS
Silas stood straight, his eyes better adjusted to the dark room, and saw a monster mask on a shelf … It was familiar, a zombie. "That mask," he said … "Where'd you get it?"	293.7–15	Silas has suspicions about Wallace and by the time he enters his house he is almost certain that Wallace is responsible for shooting Larry and killing Tina, but the sight of the zombie mask is the final, unarguable proof. Silas remembers the mask very clearly and knows perfectly well that it belongs to Larry.
French came in the room … He had a large plastic bag with what looked like a severed head inside. Larry's mask. "Can you identify this?" "Yeah," Larry said. "It's mine." "You'll get it back." "I don't want it. Just throw it away."	297.27–298.16	The last appearance of the mask. It had become a symbol for Larry of Wallace and of his own monstrosity (however unfair). But now that Wallace has died and Larry understands that it was Wallace who shot him and killed Tina, the mask is no longer charged with symbolic energy. It is simply an ugly piece of plastic which can only remind him of terrible things (being shot) and betrayals (the disillusionment of the Halloween party), and it is simply another relic from a life that has been wasted under the shadow of secrets and betrayals.

Symbols of horror: Snakes

The snake is a very ancient symbol, often associated in Christian culture with **evil, temptation and the powers of darkness** (Satan takes the form of a serpent to tempt Eve in the Garden of Eden). In other, older cultures they are associated with wisdom and knowledge of death and the underworld. They are thus not necessarily always evil, but are considered to be **creatures of darkness, mystery and otherworldly knowledge**. Due to the fact that they shed their skins and emerge from the remains of their former "bodies",

3.5   Themes

snakes are also a potent and ancient symbol of rebirth. This idea is relevant to the redemption of both Larry and Silas, as they both manage to shed the "skin" of their former lives and move on as new men.

Snakes in *Crooked Letter*

Snakes appear many times in the novel. They are hidden in letterboxes, hunted by the boys (Larry and Silas) in the woods, often mistaken for being more dangerous or venomous than they actually are, and kept by both Larry and Wallace. Their strongest associations with specific characters are with Larry and Wallace, both of whom have a fascination with and an affinity for these symbolically charged reptiles. Both Wallace and Larry assemble herpetariums, which are habitats for snakes and lizards, like a fish tank or terrarium. Silas recalls Larry showing him how to do this (p. 187.22–24).

To get attention

Larry uses snakes to get attention. He knows that other kids at school will be scared, disgusted, admiring, fascinated – any reaction would be good. He just wants the attention.

Wallace is repeatedly associated with snakes. When Silas first encounters him he has a pillowcase used for catching snakes. When Irina tells Silas about Evelyn and Wallace, the key point is the fact that **he collects snakes**. And when Silas has the final showdown at Wallace's house, he is surrounded by Wallace's snakes (pp. 289–295).

When he was an outsider at school, Larry was infamous for his association with snakes: "He used to bring stuff to school, snakes he'd catch" says Silas (p. 178.23–24), and the waitress Shaniqua says her mother went to school with him: "She say that boy used to always have snakes in his pocket." (p. 181.20–21) When Larry hunts them he catches them by trapping them with a forked stick behind the head and then stuffing them into a pillowcase (p. 101.6–10). Larry teaches Silas about snakes (pp. 87–88). Wallace also collects his snakes in a pillowcase – something Silas sees (p. 191.9–10) but

3.5 Themes

initially fails to recognise for what it is. The significance only later dawns on him.

Snakes are not agents of death or violence here in the novel – no one is hurt or killed by a snake bite – but they represent menacing omens. There are harmless and venomous snakes throughout the book, but until they have been identified, they always suggest a threat, the risk of harm. On **the night of Cindy's disappearance**, the last time she is seen alive by Larry (and the reader), a black snake appears on the road in front of the car she is driving and she runs it over (pp. 163.31–164.1). Larry notices the dead snake again when he drives away from her as she runs into the night to meet her secret boyfriend.

Menacing omens

And finally, there is a snake connection in the **title of the book**. The "crooked letter" of the title suggests a snake not only in its form – the letter "s" – but also in the sibilance of the letter itself, the hissing of a serpent.

The "crooked letter"

Redemption

One of the major story arcs through the novel is about Silas and his **journey to redemption** for the damage he has caused Larry. He has to acknowledge, accept and confess to what he has done in order to free himself from the burden of his guilt and move forward with his life. Much of the initial phases of this process have been looked at in the sections above on **Memory, secrets and the past** and **Guilt, responsibility and betrayal**. We will look here briefly at the latter stages of Silas' arc towards redemption.

Silas

3.5   Themes

TEXT	PP.	ANALYSIS
He longed to … mow his way back to the boy he'd been and do it differently with Larry, go to the police and say "She was with me." What's missing out of you, Silas? Courage, he thought.	251.4–11	Silas has to redeem himself for his betrayal of Larry. This is a process. From unarticulated feelings of guilt early on in the novel, to the acknowledgment of that guilt after Angie pushes him to tell her the truth, Silas has arrived at a point here in this passage where he can allow himself to feel the sadness and shame. All he must now do is find the courage to confess.
"I been in law enforcement a long stretch now, and the one thing I can tell you for sure is that the only way you'll ever feel better about this is to own up and pay the price."	262.3–6	Roy French knows that you have to confess to escape guilt. He is here trying to pressure Larry into confessing to what French believes to be the truth (that Larry is guilty of killing Tina and tried to shoot himself). French is correct in the substance of what he's saying, but ironically, he is addressing the wrong man. The next time he tries this approach with Larry…
"Tell us the rest. It's time, Larry. Like I said, it ain't going away, this guilt." "It wasn't him," Silas said. "Is there something you want to say, then?" French asked. "It was me," he said.	265.24–266.34	… it's Silas who confesses. The confession frees Larry from all suspicion, retroactively exonerates him for the disappearance of Cindy Walker, and allows Silas to drop the burden of guilt he has been carrying and attempt to make things right with Larry. Avenging Larry (and Tina) by confronting Wallace is a form of penance he performs as he tries to atone for what he has done to Larry over the years. By the end of the novel the two men – friends and brothers – have begun to rebuild their friendship, marking the redemption of Silas Jones.

3.6 Style and Language

SUMMARY

Crooked Letter is a third person narrative told from the perspectives of the two main characters. The narrative moves back and forth between the present day and the protagonists' childhood in the late 1970s and early 80s. The language of the novel is vivid, particularly in the use of the regional dialect in the dialogue and in the effective use of striking poetic turns of phrase.

Two aspects of the style and language used in *Crooked Letter* are immediately remarkable: the **regional accents** in the dialogues and the effective use of **poetic similes and expressive imagery** in the prose.

The novel is set in a small rural community in Mississippi and the speech of most of the characters reflects a "country" manner of speaking which includes many idiosyncrasies of grammar and pronunciation. This accent is most strongly heard in Wallace Stringfellow's voice, and less so in a character like Roy French. The use of such a strong regional dialect in the novel further roots the story in a specific place – already a function of the novel's title – and gives the novel a cohesive and authentic tone (pp. 15–16 in the novel provide a brief overview of the dialect).

Rural community

The **colourful and poetic similes and imagery** used throughout the novel enhance the atmosphere of a crime thriller, which relies just as much on a brooding, melancholy atmosphere as it does on suspense and tension.

3.6   Style and Language

There are other notable stylistic devices used throughout the novel, including a **liberal use of irony** to highlight certain themes and events.

Different voices

Dialect

When Wallace speaks we can hear a barely articulate rural voice, with an accent so thick that the language is hard to understand. Larry, also a rural kid with an accent, speaks more correctly. Silas, streetwise and untrusting, has a much more curt and cautious voice.

When French and Sheriff Lolly confront Larry in the hospital, trying to pressure him into confessing, we have one of the longest sustained passages of direct speech in the novel (pp. 257–262). The two men are pressuring Larry with language and the authority and confidence of their positions, trying to confuse him, make him less certain of the truth of what he knows in order to make him agree to their version of the truth.

Vivid similes and symbolic imagery

Gothic atmosphere

Franklin uses vivid similes and poetic descriptions to enhance atmosphere and provides striking images to highlight moments in the novel. By providing sensually-charged, eye-catching images, the prose of the novel further enriches **the impression of place**: "…bursts of smoke that hung on the still air like sheets on a line" (p. 94.19–20), for example, captures the heavy, still feel of the Mississippi night, and the "dark elbow of smoke" (p. 76.10) rising from the cabin's chimney adds an oddly organic, even monstrous impression to the secretive cabin in the woods. And Larry's mother's wind chimes play "delicate notes too tender to be metal, more like soft bone on wire: he'd always thought the chime sounded like a skeleton playing a guitar" (p. 214.18–20), a prettily macabre image which deepens the novel's Southern Gothic atmosphere.

3.6 Style and Language

Franklin makes use of **ominous similes and images** to foreshadow bad things approaching. This can be seen in the opening chapter with Larry seeing bad weather approaching: "Storm clouds like a billowing mountain loomed over the northernmost trees, already the wind picking up, the chime singing from the porch (p. 19.22–24). This is before he is shot, and **the approaching storm is symbolic**. The use of pathetic fallacy – describing natural objects, features and events in terms of human emotion and behaviour – adds to the impression of something darker than just bad weather. The storm clouds "loomed" on the horizon, suggesting a menace which is more than natural. Further ominous similes are used when describing Larry and Cindy:

Foreshadowing

→ "Larry recited his shop number, slowly, as if he were giving the code to disarm a bomb." (p. 96.24–25)
→ Cindy walks with "her belly in, as if waiting to absorb a blow". (p. 242.29)

The literary techniques here associate Larry with explosive danger and Cindy with victimisation and violence, adding in both cases to the impression of dread and violence which haunts the characters. The vivid and poetic imagery provides a tone and contributes to the atmosphere of the novel. Some passages, though, serve a larger purpose in **illuminating the characters and themes of the novel**. Here is a brief look at a few prime examples.

Atmosphere

3.6   Style and Language

TEXT	PP.	ANALYSIS
Larry passed him where he sat and moved along the porch in the familiar darkness and opened the door and reached inside and clicked on the switch and flooded the night with light.	219.22–24	Shocked and disturbed by Wallace telling him about his violent sexual fantasies, Larry realises he is face to face with a real monster. He steps out of the "familiar darkness" and lets in the light. This symbolic passage shows us the deep divide between the real monster (Wallace) and the lonely outsider (Larry), and shows us that despite his familiarity with the darkness, Larry is a good man, an agent of light.
He moved his hand to the center of the table. He hoped she'd place hers on top of it, but she didn't. He looked out the window where he could see their reflections, saw her watching him and focused on her profile, it was easier than looking at her eyes, seeing what she must be thinking.	249.8–11	Silas is often caught in symmetries in the novel. We see here how he is literally unable to look his girlfriend in the eye, symbolising how unwilling and unable he is to confront his own past and guilt.
…now that the lightning had been unleashed, so much, so often, the world seemed weirdly strobe-lit, at odds with itself, day and night battling for dominion like God and the devil.	278.15–20	The storm symbolises the crisis which is unfolding on different levels: Silas' hunt for the real killer, Larry's struggle with the world and his knowledge of what Wallace may be capable of, and Silas' struggles with his guilt.

3.6   Style and Language

TEXT	PP.	ANALYSIS
It was country dark, as Alice Jones had called these nights, the absence of any light but what you brought to the table.	321.27–28	A vivid symbol for the lonely melancholy stillness of rural Mississippi, this "country dark" night is the essence of the atmosphere of the Southern Gothic literary genre. There is a suggestion of menace and morbidity in the darkness, but the hope or whisper of companionship, human warmth and community in the light being brought to the table.

Symbols: The mask and the cabin

These two potent objects are deeply symbolic. The cabin in particular represents the **hidden past**, the secrets of Silas' origins, Carl's guilt, Larry and Silas' friendship and the fight between them, and of course Wallace's crime. It is a dark and uncomfortable place, located deep in the woods owned by Carl Ott. Later, 25 years after the disappearance of Cindy Walker and the fight between Larry and Silas, it is being reclaimed by the woods, its secrets being buried ever deeper by and within the land itself – Silas has the impression that the cabin is being "digested" by the woods (p. 193.12–17).

The cabin

When Silas discovers the body of Tina Rutherford, the cabin is fiercely illuminated and meticulously searched by the investigators. All its secrets are dragged out into the light and the cabin is briefly pulled back out of nature's grasp, "illuminated that night by harsh floodlights" (p. 224.27).

The mask represents the monstrous. A realistic zombie mask which Larry mail-ordered as a child, it has **different functions** throughout Larry's life. Chronologically, for Larry, it's an exciting toy which grants him a brief **moment of popularity** at school and the illusion of friendship and belonging, when he is invited to join

The zombie mask

3.6 Style and Language

in a Halloween haunted house party. Later, he uses it as a **tool to scare off Wallace** when the boy is prying around on Larry's property. And finally, as far as Larry is concerned, it is the last thing he sees when he is shot – **Wallace is wearing the mask**.

In the other timeline of the book, the chronology of the narrative that we as readers experience, we first encounter it when Larry is shot by an unknown figure hiding behind the zombie mask. **The mask appears again and again throughout the narrative**, always in flashbacks, until the showdown between Silas and Wallace. When Silas sees **Larry's zombie mask in Wallace's house** then he knows for sure – he had been suspicious, but is now certain – that it was Wallace who shot Larry.

Irony

There are numerous instances of irony in the book which are used for humorous or subversive purposes. Here are a few examples.

TEXT	PP.	ANALYSIS
She clicked on the radio and began turning the dial, settling on a station playing the Bee Gees' 'Stayin' Alive'.	161.13	This is the last evening of Cindy's life before being (presumably) murdered by her step-father. The mention of the song title is a cruel irony.
…kids flocked around him… Larry must've felt almost normal… .	178–179	The irony here in the Halloween party scene is that the gorily realistic zombie mask provides Larry with his only brief moment of belonging to school society. Only by putting on the face of a monster can the very un-monstrous Larry be accepted by other people. Later, with no mask and no protection, he becomes "Scary Larry".

3.6 Style and Language

TEXT	PP.	ANALYSIS
[Roy French urging Larry to confess]	260–265	French is pressuring Larry to confess by repeatedly reminding him how unbearable unconfessed guilt can be. Of course it's Silas, not Larry, he should be addressing, and in the end when all three are present and French is directly addressing Larry, it's Silas who responds, to the great surprise of everyone.

3.7 Interpretations

SUMMARY

Crooked Letter is a crime thriller – it was marketed as such by the publishers, it can be found in the Crime Fiction sections in bookshops, and the story revolves around a crime and how that crime is solved. But as the discussion below will show, there is more than one tradition in the genre of crime fiction, and Tom Franklin's novel belongs to the more literary tradition which has developed from the works of Raymond Chandler.

Restoring symbolic order to the world

Crime fiction has long been understood to deal with the kind of crisis in the world that can be seen in ancient stories like the Old English poem *Beowulf*, where a hero must defend his people against two monsters who threaten to disturb or destroy the order of the world. These are among the most primal of all stories – the protection of the community to which storyteller and listener belong from the threat of disorder, chaos or destruction, typically manifesting in the form of an Outsider (a monster) and/or a transgression of the community's laws and values.

Order of the world   Very basically, in crime fiction the "right order" of the world is symbolically threatened or disturbed by the crime – an unnatural act which defies **right, law, order**. The protagonist – investigator, detective, police officer – serves as a **representative of the reader** and of the forces of order (very explicitly so, as protagonists in crime fiction are most often law enforcement officials or detectives). The protagonist must then *on behalf of* the reader and the forces of order attempt to **correct the imbalance** – to right the wrong, destroy the monster, and restore order to the world.

3.7 Interpretations

These are very broad **symbolic concept**s which underpin the general form and function of crime fiction. In the literary history of crime fiction we can see a clear break which is usually marked by the American writer of *noir* detective novels, **Raymond Chandler**. With the works of Chandler and his lasting influence on crime fiction we have a clear case of **before-and-after**. This can best be illustrated with a brief look at the differences between what came before, in the form of Agatha Christie, probably the most famous crime fiction writer ever, and what Chandler did to the genre.

Raymond Chandler (1888–1959)

Agatha Christie and the whodunit

Agatha Christie (1890–1976) wrote over 60 mystery or detective novels and produced 14 collections of short stories in the genre. She is world famous for her mystery and detective novels featuring either Hercule Poirot or Miss Marple. Both of these characters are unthreatening **(a short, tubby Belgian and a little old English lady, respectively)** and rely on their powers of observation and their intellects to solve the crimes they discover. The structure of Agatha Christie's most famous stories usually follows the **"closed room"** format: A murder is committed in a closed space, meaning that the murderer must be among those people present before and after the murder. Classic examples include the train in *Murder on the Orient Express* (first published in 1934) and the island in *And Then There Were None* (1939).

Hercule Poirot and Miss Marple

The novels focus on the mystery of who killed the victim, how they did it and why. For this reason this **tradition of crime fiction** is known as "whodunits" (who done, i.e. did, it). The emphasis is absolutely on the mechanics of the crime and the attempted cover up, and the genius of the detective in unravelling the mystery and exposing these mechanics. In this sense, whodunits are extremely functional narratives and are concerned above all with the intricacies and mechanics of the crime and how it is solved.

Who killed the victim – how and why?

Whodunits have not become extinct as a tradition, and it's probably safe to say that the **majority of crime shows on TV fit comfortably into this format**: Week for week the main characters encounter and solve a crime. The protagonists and the fact that a crime has been committed are the only necessities and the only stable features. By virtue of its self-imposed limitations, this is a very specific, focused and disciplined approach to storytelling.

Raymond Chandler and *noir*

Hard-boiled novels

Raymond Chandler (1888–1959) wrote seven novels in the style he established, inspired in part by forerunners like Dashiell Hammett, which is commonly called "hard-boiled" or ***noir*** (French for "black", referring to the dark tone of the stories and world they depict) detective fiction. Hard-boiled detective fiction is typically characterised by a **focus on organised crime and corruption in society**, and the protagonists are frequently very cynical men who tend towards the macho.

Cynical Philip Marlowe

Chandler's greatest creation is the **detective** Philip Marlowe, and his continuing influence on American popular fiction in particular is due to his extremely atmospheric writing style and his great gift for producing hard-hitting, realistic dialogue.

But aside from his stylistic qualities and literary talents, Chandler's largest influence may have been in transferring the focus of crime fiction from the mechanics of the crime to other concerns. The crime and the solving of the crime remain in place as a structure and as a machine to drive the plot, but this structure is now no longer the sole purpose: It has instead become an excuse to examine other issues. These might include the **psychology of criminals**, investigators and people caught up in desperate situations, or social issues such as poverty, racism, social unrest or corruption.

3.7 Interpretations

In the genre of crime or detective fiction after Raymond Chandler, the emphasis in the writing and the style is likely to be much more concerned with establishing **immersive atmospheres** and complex and ambiguous characters than with precise exposure of the mechanics of the crime. And the substance of the genre has, since Chandler, become increasingly concerned with either the collateral damage of the crime or what the crime reveals about the society or community in which it was committed.

Complex characters

How *Crooked Letter, Crooked Letter* fits in

Crooked Letter is in one way an obvious descendant of the Chandler style of using a crime as a structure which supports an investigation of other issues. In the case of *Crooked Letter*, these other issues include **the collateral damage of the original crime** (Silas' guilt and Larry's isolation) as well as the exposure of social inequality (the rich girl is avenged, the poor girl lost in obscurity) and a general look at racial and social dynamics in rural Mississippi. The crime fiction elements are definitely present, and they are definitely the driving force of the plot, but it is clear that the author's intentions are more focused on what the crime says **about the characters** around it and about the world in which it took place than he is with the "whodunit" aspect.

The style and tone of the book are also far removed from the clean-cut precision of the Agatha Christie tradition. The book is rich with **emotion and pain** and as is discussed elsewhere in this study guide, the author makes effective use of vivid and poetic imagery to enhance a strong sense of **atmosphere and place**. In both style and substance, it is clear that Tom Franklin's interest lies with his characters and their emotional and psychological makeup and development, and that the crimes provide the tools to explore them.

Emotional

4.   CRITICAL RECEPTION

SUMMARY

Crooked Letter, Crooked Letter was well received and won awards and prizes, but there were also critical reactions.

Reactions

Positive reactions

Positive critical reactions to *Crooked Letter, Crooked Letter* have drawn attention to two features of the novels – Franklin's skill at describing the region and **creating a Southern atmosphere**, and the ambition of the novel to grow beyond the limits of the genre of crime or mystery fiction.

> "There is a great sense of place and exceptional character development in this mystery."[10]

> "Edgar Award-winning author Tom Franklin returns with his most accomplished and resonant novel so far."[11]

> "Franklin's prose is startlingly beautiful … But what sticks at the end is Franklin's shattering, heart-breaking depiction of loneliness."[12]

> "Franklin seemingly sets out precisely to subvert expectations, not just mine and those of his other fans, but those of the genres in which he operates."[13]

---

10 http://www.princetonbookreview.com/book_pages/discussion/crooked-letter-crooked-letter.php
11 https://www.amazon.com/Crooked-Letter-Novel/dp/0060594667/ref=ntt_at_ep_dpi_1
12 https://www.theguardian.com/books/2011/dec/04/books-christmas-presents-thrillers-reviews
13 http://fictionwritersreview.com/review/crooked-letter-crooked-letter-by-tom-franklin

"Most mysteries barely have the horsepower to create one credible antagonist, but *Crooked Letter*, true to its doubled-down title, has a rich duality when it comes to delivering darkness. … In the best of the literary mysteries, the writing matches the plotting in excellence. Franklin's latest novel works not only because of its characters and their believability and depth, and not only because of its deadeye social realism. It works because of the poetic and controlled way the writing plays out on the page and in the mind of the reader."[14]

"He draws the south – Mississippi in *Crooked Letter*, but he's plumbed Alabama too – in a warm-hearted, sympathetic but not uncritical way that few others I've read have managed to … [he] avoids the pitfalls of judgment, generalization, or exoticizing."[15]

"This is another of the distinguishing characteristics of a great literary mystery – the setting itself becomes a character."[16]

But there have also been **critical reactions**. Some of these have had to do with Franklin's **crime fiction structure**, and the – some critics feel – unconvincing development of a plot: "Unfortunately, all the story lines in *Crooked Letter, Crooked Letter* rely heavily on huge plot leaps that the reader is expected to make along with the main characters."[17] The same reviewer goes on to describe the plotting of the novel as "sloppy, even lazy."

Critical reactions

---

14 https://www.pastemagazine.com/articles/2011/02/tom-franklin-crooked-letter-crooked-letter-review.html

15 http://fictionwritersreview.com/review/crooked-letter-crooked-letter-by-tom-franklin/

16 https://www.pastemagazine.com/articles/2011/02/tom-franklin-crooked-letter-crooked-letter-review.html

17 https://readeratlarge.com/2011/09/09/crooke-letter-crooked-letter-by-tom-franklin/

Race

One reviewer also took issue with Franklin's presentation of race, writing "There's little suspense in a novel that's most notable for its heavy-handed treatment of race."[18]

Prizes and awards

Franklin's first published work, the story collection *Poachers*, won the Edgar Award for Best Mystery Short Story in 1999. *Crooked Letter, Crooked Letter* won the Crime Writer's Association Gold Dagger Award in 2010, as well as the Los Angeles Times Book Prize.

---

18 https://www.kirkusreviews.com/book-reviews/tom-franklin/crooked-letter-crooked-letter/

5. MATERIALS

The American South

As usual, Wikipedia can be recommended as a first stop to learn the general outlines of a topic. It is a useful resource to find orientation on subjects as huge as the history of the USA, and the lists of sources are invaluable for more focussed, scholarly and detailed studies of specific topics.

The following hub pages are useful resources and can point readers to more specific and authoritative sources:

Useful Links

https://en.wikipedia.org/wiki/Southern_United_States
https://en.wikipedia.org/wiki/American_Civil_War
https://en.wikipedia.org/wiki/Racism_in_the_United_States
https://en.wikipedia.org/wiki/Racial_segregation_in_the_United
_States
https://en.wikipedia.org/wiki/Modern_display_of_the_Confederate
_flagReactions_to_2015_Charleston_church_shooting
https://en.wikipedia.org/wiki/Southern_Gothic

A brief history of the American South

The American South is more a cultural than a geographical area. The American South includes those states which formed the Confederacy during the American Civil War (1861–1865) and fought against the Union. So while it doesn't include geographically southern states like New Mexico and Arizona, it does include West Virginia, which separated from the state of Virginia during the Civil War. Another term used to describe this region is the Old South, which means specifically those states which fought a civil war to uphold the institution of slavery.

Old South

South: rural and
agricultural

Generally, the North has been a more urbanised, industrialised region, with the South being more rural and agricultural. The North is much more densely populated.

The origins and causes of the Civil War are of course very complex, but the issue of slavery was a decisive factor. The huge cotton plantations in the South were run using slave labour, and when the Republican Party in the North under Abraham Lincoln moved to abolish the spread of slavery, the largely Democratic South rebelled and formed a Confederacy of States to separate from the Northern Union.

Reconstruction
Era

The South was defeated and the Union restored, and in the following period (known as the Reconstruction Era) the South faced major social changes. Its population, resources and economy had been seriously depleted by the Civil War. New federal laws were passed giving African-Americans citizenship and voting rights, and many Northerners came south to live and work. Old Southern elites found the new structures hard to deal with and formed organisations to combat these changes, either politically or through racial terrorism.

The economic struggles of the South led to periods of mass migration, with hundreds of thousands of black Americans heading to the North. A very broad view of the history of the American South would show that the region never truly recovered from the consequences of the Civil War, either economically or socially.

The South in the 20th century

Civil Rights Movement (1960s)

The period covered in the novel (late 1970s-early 2000s) is long after the founding events of the South. This is the era immediately following the Civil Rights Movement of the 1960s, which saw an end to the enforced segregation of blacks and whites. But for communities which had for many generations lived with a certain view of the world, even decades later it is hard to escape traditions and attitudes.

The South has a strong and lasting reputation for racism and racial violence which may not be entirely fair – the North is not free of racism or white supremacist violence – but racial problems may be more widespread in the South due to their historical roots, and the ages-old resentments that have been kept alive by the cult of the Confederacy. This has become painfully apparent in recent years with the growing number of bitterly controversial arguments about removing monuments to figures from the Confederacy, many of whom were slave-owners fighting to protect the institution of slavery: the banning of the Confederate flag, which has increasingly become a symbol used by white supremacists to provoke their opponents and focus racist energies: and the resulting efforts to focus on the crimes of slavery and the racism which made it possible.

Racism and racial violence

Rural life

In small rural communities in the Deep South – the states Georgia, Alabama, South Carolina, Mississippi and Louisiana – the older generations of whites and blacks alive today will have lived through the era of segregation and the Civil Rights Movement, and will remember growing up in communities where black and white kids couldn't go to the same schools and black people couldn't be buried in white-only graveyards. This is present throughout *Crooked Letter* without being the major focus of the novel: it's just how life is in the rural South, as Franklin presents it to us.

Racial segregation

There is ambient racism throughout the rural world of the novel. It matters if you're black or white: it makes a difference. Silas' relationship with Cindy, a white girl, was almost a scandal, drawing suspicion from passers-by, and his mother forbade him to see her. His relationship with Angie – who is black – is no problem at all.

1 FORWORD –
   AT A GLANCE

2 TOM FRANKLIN:
   LIFE & WORK

3 ANALYSES AND
   INTERPRETATIONS

Larry succumbs to social pressure and makes racist taunts and uses racist insults, but he knows all the time that it's wrong and he feels terrible about it.

Southern Gothic

There have been countless studies, books and films made about the racial dynamics and tensions in the rural South. More specifically relevant to *Crooked Letter* is the subgenre of literature called Southern Gothic, which is defined by its location and a generally dark tone and choice of subject matter. Classic examples include Harper Lee's *To Kill A Mockingbird* (1960), despite its warmth and sense of hope; the novels and short fiction of Carson McCullers and Flannery O'Connor, which focus on topics like lonely outsiders and religious intensity: James Dickey, author of the famous thriller *Deliverance* (1970), about the dangers "civilised" men face in the wilderness of the South: Cormac McCarthy, whose almost Biblical seriousness and fixation on masculinity and violence was parodied by Tom Franklin in *Smonk*: Anne Rice, who reimagined the vampire myth, and most of whose best work has been set in a richly atmospheric portrayal of New Orleans: and Edgar Allan Poe, one of the most important figures in American literature.

6. SAMPLE EXAM QUESTIONS AND ANSWERS

Task 1*

Compare and contrast Larry and Silas' relationships with their mothers.

Model answer:

Ina Ott and Alice Jones are very different women. Ina is gentle, submissive and devout, and Alice is hard and strong. Ina is married and raises her son in a stable environment: Alice is driven back and forth from Mississippi to Chicago and back again, a single mother who must do what she can to provide for herself and her son. *Ina and Alice*

The two boys are shaped by their mothers. Silas takes after his mother in being hard and strong in his self-interest: he protects himself by sacrificing Larry after the disappearance of Cindy Walker. Larry in turn inherits more from his mother than from his father Carl. He is, like Ina, a basically gentle and kind person. When Alice teaches Silas to rely on himself and to be constantly aware that the world is a cold, hard, unforgiving place, Ina teaches Larry to pray and provides him with all the comfort she can, whether he is suffering from asthma or from loneliness.

Both Larry and Silas have close relationships with their mothers, but Silas' is much more conflicted and painful. Alice is strict with him, forbidding him from seeing Cindy Walker, for example, and also from playing with Larry. Ina in contrast is very indulgent with Larry, often helping to persuade Carl to allow their son to do things, like take Cindy to the movies. *Close relationships*

Silas appears to have more of Carl's nature than Larry does: he is more aggressive and more strong-willed. For example, when *Carl's nature* the two boys see Cecil and Carl harassing Cindy, it is Silas who immediately reacts and tries to protect the girl. Larry remains hidden and observes. Silas' temper and active nature show more of Carl's nature than Larry's passivity does. It is because Silas as a boy is so strong-willed and angry that he clashes with his mother so often, and grows up resenting her attempts to control him. Only later, after she has died, does he really come to understand and accept how much she had sacrificed for him and how painfully lonely and hard her life had been. Larry has no such conflict with his mother, and he remains close to her. When she is in the nursing home, lost to Alzheimer's, he continues to take every opportunity to see her.

Silas' struggles with Alice made him resent and reject her, something he feels badly about as an adult, but she had also made him strong and able to deal firmly with other people. Larry has a closer and more affectionate relationship with Ina, but her mothering has increased the meekness and passivity of his gentle nature.

Task 2**

> "What's missing out of you, Silas?" (p. 141.31)
> What does Alice mean when she says this to her son?

Model answer:

Courage and empathy

Alice is concerned that Silas lacks the courage to face life's challenges head on, but she also worries that he lacks empathy and understanding for others. When he tries to run away from her on the way south, jumping out of the truck a local man is giving Alice and Silas a lift in (pp. 138–139), she is frightened for him and then furious. She tells him that he has had a relatively good and easy life so far, and has no reason to behave as he has done. She doesn't explain herself more, and as an adult Silas is still haunted by this moment.

We can see later in the conflict Silas has within himself that it is both courage and empathy which he lacks. His refusal to tell the truth about the night Cindy disappeared can be understood to be rooted in both fear of the consequences and a lack of empathy for the incredible damage he does to Larry and the Ott family by not speaking out. When he finally does tell the truth to Roy French, it is a huge moment, made maybe even worse than it would have been by the weight of 25 years delay: by this point, Larry's life has been ruined by Silas' lack of courage and empathy.

Truth

Task 3***

> "Larry felt a strange forgiveness for him because all monsters were misunderstood." (pp. 24.22–23)
> Have Larry's feelings about monsters, and Wallace in particular, changed by the end of the novel?

Model answer:

As someone who has been shunned and ostracised for 25 years by the community he grew up in, Larry has a lot of understanding for other outsiders. He knows that he is considered a monster by everyone round him, and he is frequently the victim of vandalism and abuse by local kids who come to his farm to taunt 'Scary Larry'.

Scary Larry

At the start of the novel he has lost contact with Wallace, but, as we find out later, he has spent a fair amount of time with him, and has displayed enormous patience and understanding for a very weird and suspicious character. He sees a kinship between the two of them, cast out from normal society by circumstances largely beyond their control – Larry is innocent of what he is suspected of having done,

Wallace

1 FORWORD –
   AT A GLANCE

2 TOM FRANKLIN:
   LIFE & WORK

3 ANALYSES AND
   INTERPRETATIONS

and Wallace can't really help having been born poor and weird. It is what the two men make of their circumstances which is the key to the nature of the monsters in the novel: Larry remains a passive and gentle figure, withdrawn in isolation and doing no harm to anyone else. Wallace has something much darker in his nature, a desire to hurt and an obsession with violence, domination, sexual abuse and murder.

The inner monster

Larry tries not to judge – he tries to maintain a belief in the potential for salvation (he is a good Christian, after all) in all men, even Wallace, and even after Wallace tells him his deepest fantasies of abducting, raping and murdering young women. But after he has awoken from his coma and is being pressured by French and Sheriff Lolly to confess to crimes he never committed, he begins to understand that the monster is what is *within*, not just in how one is perceived: wearing a mask, whether it's the literal zombie mask or the figurative mask of 'Scary Larry', doesn't make you a monster. Wallace's inner demons make him a true monster, and by the end of the novel Larry has come to understand that he and Wallace are not the same kind of beast, that despite their shared experience of being outsiders, Wallace is truly monstrous because of what is within him and how he acts upon it.

SOURCES & REFERENCES

Edition used for this study guide:
Franklin, Tom: *Crooked Letter, Crooked Letter*. Stuttgart: Ernst Klett
   Sprachen, 2017.
Note: All page references are to the Klett English Edition of the
novel (ISBN 978-3-12-579900-4) and refer to the page and line
numbers: for example, 191.25 is line 25 on page 191.

About the author:
http://www.harpercollinsspeakersbureau.com/speaker/tom-
   franklin/
A Q&A with Author Tom Franklin. undated, Amazon.
   https://www.amazon.com/Crooked-Letter-Novel/
   dp/0060594667/ref=ntt_at_ep_dpi_1 → A short but highly
   informative interview with the author from amazon.com
https://www.mswritersandmusicians.com/mississippi-writers/
   tom-franklin → This article and interview dates from before the
   publication of *Crooked Letter*, and is interesting for its focus on
   his identity as a regional writer. The interview is extensive and
   filled with autobiographical details and insights into the South.

Reviews:
Charles, Ron: *Tom Franklins 'Crooked Letter, Crooked Letter.
   29.9.2010*, Washington Post. http://www.washingtonpost.com/
   wp-dyn/content/article/2010/09/28/AR2010092805310.html
   → A relatively in-depth and positive review of the novel
Flood, Alison: *Books for giving: thrillers.* 4.12.2011, The Guardian.
   https://www.theguardian.com/books/2011/dec/04/books-
   christmas-presents-thrillers-reviews → Brief and positive
   review from the UK newspaper

Kirkus Review. 14.7.2010. https://www.kirkusreviews.com/book-reviews/tom-franklin/crooked-letter-crooked-letter/ → A less positive reaction to the book

Langness, Peter: *Tom Franklin: Crooked Letter, Crooked Letter*. 7.2.2011, Paste Magazine. https://www.pastemagazine.com/articles/2011/02/tom-franklin-crooked-letter-crooked-letter-review.html → This review places *Crooked Letter* in the context of Franklin's career to that point, and paying particular attention to his status as a regional writer, or even Southern Gothic

Princeton Book Review: *Crooked Letter, Crooked Letter*. By Tom Franklin. Undated. http://www.princetonbookreview.com/book_pages/discussion/crooked-letter-crooked-letter.php

Tolmsted: *Crooked Letter, Crooked Letter by Tom Franklin*. 9.9.2011, Reader at Large. https://readeratlarge.com/2011/09/09/crooke-letter-crooked-letter-by-tom-franklin/ → This review looks at the good and bad sides of the novel.

Wetherell, Brad: *Crooked Letter, Crooked Letter*, by Tom Franklin. 21.12.2011, Fiction writers Review. http://fictionwritersreview.com/review/crooked-letter-crooked-letter-by-tom-franklin/ → Another lengthy and positive review

Useful Links by Wikipedia:
About Southern Gothic fiction:
https://en.wikipedia.org/wiki/Southern_Gothic

About the Southern United States:
https://en.wikipedia.org/wiki/Southern_United_States

About the American Civil War:
https://en.wikipedia.org/wiki/American_Civil_War

About Racism in the United States of America:
https://en.wikipedia.org/wiki/Racism_in_the_United_States
https://en.wikipedia.org/wiki/Racial_segregation_in_the_United
 _States
https://en.wikipedia.org/wiki/Modern_display_of_the_Confederate
 _flag#Reactions_to_2015_Charleston_church_shooting

(Links last accessed on 6.12.2017)

INDEX

DIGITALES ZUSATZMATERIAL

Literarisch vernetzt! Über 600 Materialien online.